A BIBLE READING GUIDE

FOR

BIBLE READING PEOPLE

The Study of the Bible in Chronological Sequence

This approach to Bible study, with its "Reflections on Readings" will provide for many a new approach for reading and understanding the Word of God. The sequence of the readings are taken from the "Chronological Bible", printed by E.E.Gaddy and Associates: Editor Ed. Reese.

The purpose of the "Chronological Bible" is to take "all the events of the Bible, rearrange them in the order in which they happen, and record them in the chronological order." This reading guide, however, will prove beneficial with any translation of your choice.

The purpose of this Bible Reading Guide, with its "Reflections on Readings", is to make your reading of the Bible, chronologically, more beneficial for personal devotion and Bible class study. The "Reflections on Readings" can be discussed in class setting or reviewed in personal devotions. Other brief aids are offered from time to time to add to the enlightenment and understanding of the daily readings.

This Bible Reading Guide is designed as a three-year study venture. I pray the Holy Spirit to bless your spirit as you diligently "Search the Scriptures."

Leo E.Wehrspann
1989

****

A BIBLE READING GUIDE -
        for BIBLE READING PEOPLE -

GOAL -- To read the entire Scripture through - CHRONOLOGICALLY - in the period of three (3) years. [Approximately one (1) chapter a day - seven (7) chapters a week.]

"Let the Word of Christ dwell in you richly"

****

IMPORTANT TO KNOW as you begin this venture. This arrangement of Bible reading leads you through the Scripture in the step-by-step order of how and when the events occurred. This will provide more continuity of thought, but it will necessitate referring to different chapters and verses in the same day's reading. It will be helpful if you put the date in the margin of your Bible when you read the various texts. It will add to your interest and make later cross references easier to use.

This approach to Bible study is called the "Inductive Method" of Bible Study. Read the Bible with an open spirit and permit the Holy Spirit to speak through the WORD as you contemplate its meaning.

As you read the portion of Scripture assigned, look for and jot down in a notebook impressions that you gain from your reading. Then share with others the thoughts of the Spirit that have come to you. Use the following questions to prompt your deliberation.

The Book or portion of the Bible you are studying:_____
Chapter_____ Verse (s)_____

1. What are the important words or concepts that impress you?

2. What are the doctrinal truths that come to your attention?

3. What are some problems or verses which you think need explanation?

4. What would you choose as the key verse in this section?

5. Are there other verses important to remember?

6. Do you recall other portions of Scripture that speak of the same subject matter? (A concordance is helpful to locate parallel passages.)

7. What practical application would you make for your personal life and the life of all Christians?

8. How would you summarize the section into a general heading?

9. What general outline would you make of the section you have studied?

10. Where and how do you see LAW/GOSPEL content in what you have read?

****

CONCEPTS FOR BIBLE STUDY:

As the Scriptures unfold, keep in mind the following:

THE SCRIPTURE IS:

I. A Book of doctrine to which we ascribe fundamentals of belief effecting our relationship with God. e.g.-CREATION: We say unequivocally, "I believe in God, the Father, Almighty, CREATOR of heaven and earth." This cannot be denied without effecting our relationship with God as the authoritative source of all life and light and all things that exist.

II. A Book of detail which explains the how and what of the circumstances involved. There is often disagreement about the detail. This does not effect the doctrine. In the explanation of detail, variation of opinion must be allowed within the framework of the doctrine. e.g. "Where did Cain and Abel find wives for themselves -- or length of days of creation- or where did light come from?

-2-

The sequence of happenings for the first eleven chapters of Genesis:

> The Creation
> The Fall of Man
> The Beginning of Violence (Cain and Abel)
> The Vast Wickedness of Earth
> The Flood
> The Promise
> The Altar
> The Names and Descendants of a Spreading Population
> The Tower of Confusion

Important Concepts to Consider:

The Purpose of Creation: Genesis 1:26--2:4.
The Problem of Fear: Genesis 3:10 (Revelations 1:17-18).
(Fear and how we deal with it, and how God relieves it, is an over-arching theme in the Bible, overshadowing all other pre-dominant themes.)
The importance of personal responsibility: Gen. 1:27-28; 3:11-13
The concept of the TREE:
>   Gen. 2:9: The TREES of the GARDEN
>   John 3:14: The TREE of the CROSS
>   Rev. 22:2: The TREE of LIFE
The woman as progenitor of all Christians (Gen. 3:13-15;
>   Gal. 4:4; Rev. 12:1-6)
The Balance of the Message:

LAW	GOSPEL
Driven from the Garden	Promise of deliverance through the woman's seed
Judgement of Cain	Protection from oppression
Judgement through the Flood	"Never Again" - The rainbow of Promise
Destruction of the Tower	The Messianic People: The Hebrews

****

Add these thoughts to your reading:

1. Make personal notes in the margins as you read your Bible.
2. You may appreciate underlining in color:
   RED --- Salvation; Redemption; Passages of Promise (GOSPEL).
   BLACK -- Sentences of judgment and expression of God's disfavor (LAW).
   BLUE --- Passages reflecting loyalty to God and guidance through His Spirit (Obedience to God).
   GREEN -- Miscellaneous passages of information, history, etc.
3. Read and study with an ear open for the Spirit's message:
   a) What is God saying?
   b) What does it mean?
   c) Does it have personal application for me in my life today?
4. In your notebook, jot down questions which come to your mind that can be shared in group discussion.
5. Do not expect to understand everything you read the first time through.

6. Check off each day's reading as you progress. You will then be able to return and make up the days that have been missed.

7. Take special note of the key thoughts suggested with this guide. They will help your personal meditation and understanding of what you read.

****

LET'S BEGIN TO SHARE

BIBLE READING GUIDE
    for BIBLE READING PEOPLE

✓January 1 - "In the Beginning"   John 1:1-2; Psalm 90:2;
                                    Genesis 1:1; Isaiah 14:12-17;
                                    Ezekiel 28:13-26; Genesis 1:2a;
                                    Jeremiah 4:23-26; Isaiah 45:18

        2 - God said and God made   Genesis 1:2b-8; 2:5-6;
                                    1:9-26; 2:7

        3 - God made MAN and WOMAN Genesis 5:1; 1:27; 2:18-25;
                                    5:2; 3:20; 1:28-31; 2:1-4;
                                    John 1:3; Exodus 20:11

        4 - From Paradise to Predicament   Genesis 2:8-17; 3:1-19;
            (one easy lesson)   3:21-24

        5 - Families and family problems   Genesis 4:1-15

        6 - From Generation to Generation   I Chronicles 1:1; Genesis
                                    4:16-25; 5:3; 4:26; 5:6; 5:9;
                                    Genesis 5:12; 5:15; 5:18

        7 - Death and Life - in the hands   I Chronicles 1:3; 1:27;
                 of God   Genesis 5:21; 5: 4-5

****

REFLECTIONS ON READINGS

January 1 through January 7

Discuss or contemplate the relation between Genesis 1:1-2 with John 1:1-4 & vs.14

Important concepts to consider:
        The power of God in creation
        The perspective of marriage and companionship -- Genesis 2:18
        The FALL and the FEAR that resulted -- Genesis 3:10; Rev. 1:18

        Who is responsible? Genesis 3:11-13; 4:1-15

        The significance of the TREES -- Genesis 2:9; Revelation 22:2;
            Compare Genesis 3:13-15 with Galatians 4:4-5; Rev.12:1-6

```
**********************************************************************************
```

January 8 – What God saw and said!   Genesis 5:32; 6:1-22

     9 – And the floods came   Genesis 7:1-24; 8:1-12

    10 – LAND again   Genesis 8:13-22; 9:6-17; 9:1-7

    11 – Population Explosion   Genesis 9:18-19; 10:32; 10:1-5
                               I Chron. 1:5-7; Genesis 10:20;
                               I Chron. 1:8-16; Genesis 10:31;21-23;
                               I Chron. 1:17; 24; Genesis 11:10

    12 – Too much merrymaking   Genesis 9:20-27; 11:12; 10:24; 11:14;
                               I Chron.1:18-19 & 25; Genesis 10:25-30
                               Genesis 11:18&20; I Chron.1:20-23

    13 – Man proposes, God disposes   Genesis 11:1-9; 11:22; 24; 26;
                               Job 1:1-5; Genesis 11:19; 25;
                               Genesis 9:28-29; 11:27

    14 – God's man stands firm   Job 1:6-22; 2:1-13

```
**********************************************************************************
```

REFLECTIONS ON READINGS

January 8 through January 14

How do you react personally to God's "apology" for creating man and His expression of regret? Genesis 6:5-7

What do you think Noah had that the rest of mankind did not have? Reflect on Genesis 8:20

Discuss whatever questions may be on your mind concerning "the flood".

Discuss problems of "population explosion", e.g. Genesis 10:31; Compare 11:1.

Discuss the proposition, "Man proposes, God disposes", in the light of the Tower of Babylon -- Genesis 11:1-9

```
**********************************************************************************
```

THE JOB STORY

The Book of instruction in dealing with the psychological, emotional, and spiritual relations with <u>other people.</u>

Compare - Romans (New Testament) - The Book of instruction on understanding the internal psychological, emotional and spiritual realities within one's self. Discuss, if possible, your relationship with family, friends, and those in fellowship with these perspectives in mind.

```
************************************************************************
```

January 15 - Out of the depths, we cry   Job 3 & 4

    16 - Comforting friends?   Job 5 & 6

    17 - Restless days and sleepless   Job 7 & 8
         nights

    18 - The shadows of life   Job 9 & 10

    19 - The wicked often prosper -   Job 11 & 12
         a puzzle!

    20 - The mystery of life & death   Job 13 & 14

    21 - Despair!!   Job 15 & 16

```
************************************************************************
```

REFLECTIONS ON READINGS

January 15 through January 21

Discuss the following summarization of the <u>Book</u> <u>of</u> <u>Job</u>.

<u>Summarization</u>: What do we learn about suffering and healing from the Book of
               Job?

1. There is not always an answer as to the reason for suffering in a
    person's life.

2. There is not always a correlation between suffering and the cause
    of suffering.

3. There is not always a correlation between suffering and the goodness
    or the badness of an individual. Wicked people may suffer because of
    their wickedness. Christian people may suffer even though they are
    not wicked. Wicked people may never suffer in all their lifetime, and
    Christian people may suffer extreme hardship and sickness and difficulty.

4. Good righteous people suffer illness, though unexplainably.

5. There are many forms of suffering. Job's suffering was not only phy-
    sical, not only the loss of property, but he suffered the loss of
    family, the loss of friends, the loss of fellowship with his wife. All
    of this happened to a good righteous man. Likewise, there are many
    forms of healing. Those who see healing only in physical terms often
    miss the greater dimensions of healing that take place emotionally and
    spiritually.

6. Christians do not always have the perfect hold on life, seemingly.
    They suffer depression, frustration, and even the emotion of anger
    against God.

7. Christians suffer the breakdown of human relationships even as non-Christians do.

8. To try to comfort a person by saying, "It's God's will", is of little comfort to that person. To say, "God is punishing you", is even more disastrous.

9. Christians do have a power to cope with problems that can be utilized for their benefit, _if_ they use the resources in Christ and the Spirit that are available to them.

10. The final solution to suffering is not always conquering of the dreadful evil or sickness or affliction which attacks us, but the final <u>confidence is to know Jesus Christ</u>, and the ultimate assurance of perfect justice and overcoming all sickness and affliction in the life everlasting. (I John 3:2ff)

****

January 22	– Hope for the future	Job 17, 18, 19
23	– Triumph for the ungodly doesn't last	Job 20, 21
24	– A reason for testing	Job 22, 23
25	– God's vision – "20/20" – He sees ALL	Job 24, 25, 26
26	– The hypocrite will not be spared	Job 27, 28
27	– Reminiscence and Remembrance	Job 29, 30
28	– Why? Why? Why?	Job 31
29	– The voice of youth is worth listening to	Job 32, 33
30	– God is always fair	Job 34
31	– Look to the heavens	Job 35, 36

****

REFLECTIONS ON READINGS

January 22 through January 31

SOME GENERAL ANSWERS TO: WHY SICKNESS? – WHY SUFFERING?

1. Because of the human condition since the Fall. If there had been no sin, there would be no sickness and death.

2. A testing for our benefit.

3. A strengthening of our personal faith.

4. An opportunity for our own witness.

5. Because of other people's misbehavior that may cause our suffering and have no relation to our personal sins and shortcomings. "They have persecuted ME; they will also persecute you." (John 15:20)

6. Because of our stupidity, e.g. over-drinking, bad eating habits.

7. For the purpose of strengthening others.

8. Totally unexplainable. There is seldom a relationship between a known reason and a consequent suffering.

9. It may be an opportunity for God to show His power and glory in healing. (John 9:1-3)

10. The ultimate answer is always faith--faith that "God works for good for all who love Him." (Romans 8:18ff)

ADDENDA:

Much truth is spoken through the mouths of misguided persons. Much falsehood may be expressed by very righteous and deserving people.

Always apply I Thessalonians 5:19-21, recognizing our own fallibility, yet leaning on the Spirit for growing Truth and utilizing the fellowship to share and to test varying opinions.

****

BIBLE READING GUIDE
for BIBLE READING PEOPLE

February 1 - God's still in control	Job 37 & 38
2 - Great God, little man	Job 39 & 40
3 - Does God owe me anything?	Job 41
4 - The Lord can turn it all around.	Job 42: 1-17
Abram and all of his	Gen. 11:21-23; 11:28-32; 12:1-3
5 - The calls and promises of God	Gen. 14:1-4; 12:4-9; Gal. 3:17; Gen. 12:10-20; 13:1-4
6 - Separations, strife, & restoration	Gen. 13:5-18; 14:5-24
7.- Faith leads to peace	Gen. 15:1-21; 16:1-16

****

February 1 through February 7

Discussion continues on the Book of Job and the guidelines: Why sickness?
     Why suffering?

Return to the genealogy of God's people.
     Discuss the Call of God: Gen. 12:1; the Promise of God: Gen. 12:2-3.
     Discuss Abram's response: Gen. 12:4-9.
          What significance do you find to Abram's action in "building altars"?
          What meaning does that have for us in following the call of Christ?

Consider some New Testament passages which reflect on Abram: Ro. 4:1-25;
          Gal. 3:6-18.

Reflect also on Abram's sin: Gen. 12:10-20.

Discuss the early problems of family strife: Gen. 13 & 14.
     On Melchizedek, High Priest: Compare Heb. 7:1-22.

What significant lessons are there to learn from these experiences?
     Consider also Gen. 15 & 16.

The earliest mention of tithing: Gen. 14:20.

****

February 8 - A New Name	Gen. 17:1-27
9 - Positive and Negative predictions	Gen. 18:1-33
10 - Take God's warnings seriously	Gen. 19:1-29
11 - Deceptions lead nowhere	Gen. 20:1-18; 21:1-7; I Chron. 1:34; Gen. 19:30-38
12 - Conflicts - Conceptions	Gen. 21:8-21; 25:12-16; I Chron. 1:29-31; Gen. 21:22-34
13 - The faithfulness of God's great man	Gen. 22:1-24; 23:1-20
14 - God's Promise continues and continues	Gen. 24

****

REFLECTIONS ON READINGS

February 8 through February 14

What's in a name? Gen. 17. Compare Is. 62:2; also vs. 4 and 12.

Also Rev. 2:17; 3:12

The fulfillment of the promise begins: Gen. 18:1-5.

What shall we do with those wicked cities? Gen. 18:1-16ff.; Gen. 19.

The temptation to deception runs strong: Gen. 20:8-14.

The beginnings of serious conflict: Gen. 21:9-32.
     Ishmael - Isaac   The test of faith: Gen. 22:1-24.
     Abimelech - Abraham The prototype of the "Only Son".

God's promise continues in the second generation: Gen. 24.

****

February 15	The Patriarch and posterity – Abraham	Gen. 25:1-11; I Chron. 1:32-33; Gen. 25:17-26; I Chron. 1:28
16	Hard times: In-law problems	Gen. 25:27-34; 26:34-35; 26:1-16
17	A truce among tribes	Gen. 26:17-33
18	A gracious father deceived	Gen. 27:1-46
19	Of visions and pledging	Jacob's line: Gen. 28:1-5; 10-22 Esau's line: Gen. 28:6-9; 36:1-30
20	Labor relations and love's illusions	Jacob's line: Gen. 29:1-20 Esau's line: I Chron. 1:35-42
21	Jealousies in human relationships	Jacob's line: Gen. 29:21-34 30:1-6; 29:35 Esau's line: Gen. 36:31-33; I Chron. 1:43-44

****

REFLECTIONS ON READINGS

February 15 through February 21

The patriarch dies; the beginning of posterity: Gen. 25; I Chron. 1:28-33.

Hard times and in-law problems: Gen. 26 & 27.
     The Promise reiterated: Gen. 26:4.

A holy vision and a tremendous response: Gen. 28.
     Discuss today's Christian's response in comparison to Jacob's experience.

A labor relations problem: Gen. 29.

Family problems, too: Gen. 30:1-6.

```
************************************************************************
```

February 22 - The "strain" of families   Jacob's line: Gen. 30:7-24;
             through generations   Esau's line: Gen. 36:34-43
                                                             I Chron.1:45-54

        23 - Work, work, and more work   Gen. 30:25-43

        24 - When God says, "Move", MOVE!   Gen. 31:1-16

        25 - Mizpah: A farewell greeting   Gen. 31:17-55

        26 - A lesson in humility   Gen. 32:1-23

        27 - Love conquers hate -   Gen. 32:24-32; 35:10; 33:1-16
             Powerful Reconciliation

        28 - While you're building--   Gen. 33:17-20
             build an altar

```
************************************************************************
```

REFLECTIONS ON READINGS

February 22 through February 28

Discuss and share views--"Strains" on family unity: Gen. 30:7-21.

A labor agreement--When God says, "Go": Gen. 31. Compare Gen. 12:1-3.

A fond farewell, Mizpah: Gen. 31:48-49.

Love conquers hate: Gen. 32: 33:1-6.

Discuss personal experiences of "wrestling" with God.

First and foremost in the mind of God's people:
        While you are building--build an ALTAR. Gen. 33:20.

```
************************************************************************
```

BIBLE READING GUID
    for BIBLE READING PEOPLE

March 1 - Treachery and retaliation   Gen. 34

      2 - Wherever you go, BUILD AN ALTAR   Gen. 35:1-19; 48:7; 35:20-27;
                                             Gen. 37:1

      3 - Dangers of parental favoritism   Gen. 37:2-36; 39:1

March 4 - A saint among the patriarchs   Gen. 38:1-5; I Chron. 2:3
          of God   Gen. 39:2-23

      5 - Special powers from special   Gen. 40:1-23; 35:28-29
          dreams

      6 - UP the ladder you must go!   Gen. 41:1-27

      7 - Prosperity and plenty   Gen. 41:28-57

****

REFLECTIONS ON READINGS

March 1 through March 7

The problem of rape is nothing new: Gen. 34.
    Discuss the current problem in comparison to the Gen. 34 account.

The predominance of the altar in the mind of God and His people: Gen. 35.
    Compare Gen. 32:22ff., also.

The dangers of parental favoritism and brotherly jealousy: Gen. 37.

Standing strong in the face of temptation: Gen. 39.

Special blessings to one of God's saints: Gen. 40 & 41.

****

March 8 - Sinners among the patriarchs,   Gen. 38:6-30; I. Chron. 2:4
          too!

      9 - A time for vengeance is   Gen. 42:1-38
          precluded by love

     10 - Brothers out, Brothers in,   Gen. 43:1-34
          RECONCILIATION

     11 - Your sins will find you out   Gen. 44:1-34

     12 - Love dispels fear   Gen. 45:1-28

     13 - Reunion with rejoicing   Gen. 46:1-28; Exodus 1: 1-5

     14 - Getting settled in a   Gen. 46:29-34; 47:1-21
          strange land

REFLECTIONS ON READINGS

March 8 through March 14

Sinners among God's people?...YES! Gen. 38.
   Even among the Patriarchs!
      Discuss the concept of sin in the lives of Christians:
      1) the cause; 2) the effect; 3) getting rid of guilt; 4) Luther's concept
      "Simul justis et peccator"...at the same time, saint (justified) and yet
      sinner).

A great example of brotherly reconciliation: Gen. 43, 44, 45, 46, 47.
   Discuss the importance of reconciliation in the life of families; the
   family of the church, etc.: Colossians 3:12-17.

****

March 15 - The promise of God goes all the way	Gen. 47:22-31; 48:1-22
16 - My Sons...	Gen. 49:1-32
17 - Father Jacob is dead...	Gen. 49:33; 50:1-21
18 - A death with grace & dignity	Ruth 4:18; I Chron. 2:5-8; Gen. 50:22-26; Ex. 1:6-7; Gen. 47:27
19 - Egypt, THE world power (1600-1200 B.C.)	Ex. 1:8-14; Num. 26:59; Ex. 6:20; 1:15-22; I Chron. 23:13
20 - Moses...a man destined to greatness	Ex. 2:1-10; 6:23; Num. 26:60; I Chron. 6:49; Ex. 2:11-15
21 - God hears the prayers of the oppressed	Ex. 2:23-25; 2:16-22; I Chron. 23:14-15; Ex. 6:25

****

REFLECTIONS ON READINGS

March 15 through March 21

The economy of a country affects also the welfare of God's people: Gen. 47-48.

A fond farewell of a stately father to his sons: Gen. 49 & 50.

Egypt, the world power: (1600 B.C.)
   How it affected God's people: Ex. 1:8-22.
   Initiation of Aaronitic Priesthood: I Chron. 23:13.

A leader emerges: A man destined to greatness...Moses: Ex. 2:1-16.

God's people under oppression: Ex.2:23-25.

    Discuss how and in what ways people of God (Christians) may experience
oppression today.

****

March 22 - A call and a commission   Ex. 3:1-22

    23 - Excuses won't do   Ex. 4:1-31

    24 - No labor union here   Ex. 5:1-23

    25 - Talk it up, Man; I'm the LORD!   Ex. 6:1-30; 7:1-7

    26 - Plagues and more plagues   Ex. 7:8-25; 8:1-7

    27 - Yet more plagues   Ex. 8:8-23

    28 - Won't they ever stop?   Ex. 8:24-32; 9:1-12

****

REFLECTIONS ON READINGS

March 22 through March 28

A call and a commission to a great work: Ex. 3.
        No excuses allowed: Ex. 4.
        Discuss how and in what way we create excuses that get in the way of
        service to the Lord.
        How and in what way has God persuaded us to serve when we make excuses?

The trauma of confrontation with Government authority: Ex. 5.
        Cite cases in which this happens in contemporary circumstances....Discuss.
        How can we be sure that God is behind a cause? Ex. 6 & 7.

The Lord can be mighty persuasive (the plagues): Ex. 7.

****

March 29 - You name it; God controls it   Ex. 9:13-35

    30 - The plagues AGAIN!   Ex. 10:1-13; 12:1-2; 10:14-20

    31 - Toughing it out with God is   Ex. 10:21-17; 11:1-8; 10:28-29;
         tough business   Ex. 11:9-10

APRIL 1 - A MEAL to be Remembered   Ex. 12:3-27

     2 - A great CRY in EGYPT   Ex. 12:28-36; 40-42;
                                            Num. 33:1-5; Ex. 12:37-39; 43-51

April 3 - Now REMEMBER THE MEAL   Ex. 13:1-22; Num. 33:6

****

REFLECTIONS ON READINGS

March 29 through April 3

More and more plagues: Ex. 8, 9, 10.
> Discuss the concept of the King's confession (Ex. 10:16-17) and his
>> stubbornness (Ex. 10:27; 11:10).
> Would you consider this a parallel to the sin against the Holy Spirit?
>> Why or why not? Refer to Matt. 12:30-32; Mark 3:28ff.; Luke 12:10ff.;
>> I John 5:16.

A concluding thought: Toughing it out with God is tough business.

A meal to be remembered, THE PASSOVER: Ex. 12:13.
> Compare Matt. 26:17ff.; Luke 22:7-14; Mark 14:12-21; John 13:21-30.
> Compare the Passover with Holy Communion.

****

April 4 - Fear not, stand still, see the salvation of the Lord!	Ex. 14:1-2; Num. 33:7; Ex. 14:3-31; Ps. 46
5 - SING the SONG of VICTORY	Ex. 15:1-21; Num. 33:8-9; Ex. 15:22-27
6 - Manna Promised - Manna Given!	Num. 33:10-11; Ex. 16:1-22; Ex. 16:31-36
7 - Take the Sabbath seriously	Ex. 16:23-30; Num. 33:12-14; Ex. 17:1-16
8 - Some good advice from a relative	Num. 33:15; Ex. 18:1-27
9 - A smoking mountain will get your attention (The Ten Commandments proclaimed)	Ex. 19:1-25; 20:1-26
10 - Laws to live by	Ex. 21:1-36

****

REFLECTIONS ON READINGS

April 4 through April 10

Let God be God: Fear not, stand still, and see the deliverance of the
> Lord: Ex. 14:13-14.

Question: Does God affect victories like this in wars today? Would you
> consider the cloud coverage of the Normandy beachhead an act of
> God similar to the Red Sea incident?

April 4 through April 10

A model song of victory: Ex. 15.
> Do we adequately and significantly give God the credit for our victories?
>   Give specific examples if you can.
> Consider Miriam's song as well as that of Moses, vs. 21.

Manna promised - Manna given: Ex. 16.
> Allowances for the Sabbath - What happened to the Sabbath in the New
>   Testament? Compare Col. 2:16ff.
> What's bread without water? Ex. 17:1-16.

In-laws can give good advice: Ex. 18.

A smoking mountain will get your attention: Ex. 19.

Discuss Ex. 20 in the light of moral law, ceremonial law, political law.
> Discuss the catechetical concepts of difference between Law and Gospel.
> 1) The law teaches what we are to do and not to do; the Gospel
>   teaches what God has done, and still does for our salvation.
> 2) The law shows our sin and the wrath of God; the Gospel shows us our
>   Savior and the grace of God.
> 3) The law must be preached to all men, but especially to impenitent
>   sinners; the Gospel must be preached to sinners who are troubled in
>   because of their sins.

Discuss law as: (a) mirror; (b) guide; (c) curb.

****

April 11 - Property rights and human rights	Ex. 22:1-31; 23:1-13
12 - Three national festivals of feasting	Ex. 23:10-33; 24:3-8
13 - In the presence of God	Ex. 24:1-2; 9-18; 25:1-22
14 - Nothing's too good for God	Ex. 25:23-30; Lev. 24:5-9; Lev. 25:31-40
15 - Nothing but the best in the sanctuary of God	Ex. 26:1-37
16 - The altar where God's people gather	Ex. 27:1-21; Lev. 24:1-4
17 - The rich and the poor before the Lord	Ex. 30:1-38

****

REFLECTIONS ON READINGS

April 11 through April 17

In relation to the week's readings, consider the following:
1) We have studied various patterns of slavery in the history of the children of Israel, e.g. Gen. 47:18-26; Ex. 5:1-19; Ex. 6:5-7; Ex. 21:1-11.
   a) What are the differences involved?
   b) Which patterns reflect the type(s) of slavery
      (1) in today's world?
      (2) in the development and growth of the United States?
   c) Who in the last 200 years, of the leaders in the contemporary world, would most typify a leader and deliverer like unto Moses?
2) Do we in today's society, (church and civil) give the same attention to justice and fairness as instructed in Ex. 23:1-9?
3) Comparative festivals: Children of Israel--
   a) Unleavened Bread: Ex. 12 and Ex. 23:14-15.
   b) Harvest Festival: Ex. 23:16.
   c) Festival of Shelters: Ex. 23:16b.

Which of today's festivals would correspond with a), b), or c)?
1) New Year's Day
2) Ash Wedesday
3) Fourth of July
4) Maundy Thursday
5) Good Friday
6) Easter
7) Trinity Sunday
8) Pentecost
9) Thanksgiving Day
10) Reformation Day?

4. As you reviewed the attention that God gave in His directions to the children of Israel in regard to:
   1) worship   2) altars   3) sanctuary
   4) offering   5) sacrifice   6) priesthood

....how do think that we compare in today's church and society? What suggestions would you make for changes, if any?

5. Are the institution and application of "blue laws" regarding Sunday labor and other laws, comparable to Sabbath laws of Old Testament practice?   Compare Ex. 31;12-17 and Colossians 2:16-23
Does this devalue or enhance the concept of worship?
Are we free to worship...privately...corporately? Heb. 10:11-25

****

April 18 - Master craftsmen - Workers in Art Ex. 31:1-11

   19 - Vesting God's servants in the   Ex. 28:1-43
        finest garments

   20 - Consecration ceremonies   Ex. 29:1-25

   21 - Offerings for the priests and   Ex. 29:26-46; 31:12-18
        by the priests

****

April 22 - Sin and anger against sin .... Ex. 32:1-35

    23 - Conversations in "church" .... Ex. 33:7-23

    24 - Conversations "under a cloud" .... Ex. 34:1-28

****

REFLECTIONS ON READINGS

April 18 through April 24

The vesting of God's servants: Ex. 28.
    Discuss the purpose of vesting of clergy, liturgical colors, and the
    purpose of paraments in the contemporary church.

What can be learned from the consecration and offering practices of God's
    people, then, and now? (Consider Ex. chapters 29--34.)

****

April 25 - Ecology, 3500 years ago! .... Lev. 25:1-34

    26 - Concern for the poor, 3500 .... Lev. 25:35-55
        years ago!

    27 - Commandments and chastisements .... Lev. 26:1-39

    28 - Promises of God and man .... Lev. 26:40-46; 27:1-25

    29 - The first-born, the first-fruit, ... Lev. 27:26-34; Ex. 34:29-35
        and the tithe, THEY ARE THE LORD'S!

    30 - Materials and labor given willingly .... Ex. 35:4-29; 36:1-7

****

REFLECTIONS ON READINGS

April 25 through April 30

Compare: 1) Ecological practices then (3500 years ago): Lev. 25:1-34, and
        today.
      2) Concern for the poor: Lev. 25:35-55.

The first-born, the first-fruits and the tithe: they are the Lord's.
        Lev. 27:26-34; Ex. 34-29-35.

For further study, consider the following:
    Leviticus and Numbers begin the heavy portions of reading in the Old
    Testament of God's Word. Several principles are necessary to be
    remembered as you read these difficult sections:

    1) As you read, try to ascertain the thrust of God's message with
        good Lutheran application of Law/Gospel distinction.

April 25 through April 30

The Law emphasis deals with:
   a) Guidance and direction.
   b) The failure of man; the problem of sin.
   c) The judgement or punishment resulting from that action.
The Gospel emphasis deals with:
   a) God's promise for the future.
   b) The expression of God's compassion.
   c) Always the Covenant of Mercy. (The Ark of the Covenant, Ex. 25:17)

As you read with this perspective in mind, the New Testament direction of Jesus (Luke 24:45-48) comes alive for contemporary problems and issues as well.

2) As you read, do not attempt to understand every passage or get the answer to every question. Follow the "Panoramic Reading" approach. Read it straight through. Let the Spirit unfold the teachings as you approach the long view and grasp the overall vision. Occasionally, we stop for the "Microscopic" approach and make a detailed study of a verse or a few verses in a more precise manner.

3) As you read, keep these questions in mind:
   a) What is God saying, or what does this passage show me about God?
   b) What does God mean by what He is saying?
   c) What is the application for me in my life today: personally, or as a church, or as a governmental community?

BRIEF OVERVIEW OF THE MAY AND JUNE READINGS:

1) The concepts of the Priesthood: Num. 3 through 8 (and 18) interwoven with Ex. 28 and 29; Lev. 7-11.

2) The concepts of Offering:
   Ex. 13:2: The first-born males, men and animals, belong to God.
   Lev. 27:30 and verses following: 1/10th of all animals and produce belong to the Lord.
   Ex. 25: Offerings for the sanctuary.
   Ex. 29:38, Num. 28:1-28: Daily offerings and burnt offerings.
   Lev. 2:6-14: Grain offerings.
   Lev. 3:7-11 and verses following: Fellowship or Peace offerings, also called Food offerings.
   Lev. 4,5,6,24: The sin offerings.
   Lev. 5:14; 7:1 and verses following: Repayment Offerings.
   Lev. 12:13: Purification offering. (Note: Luke 2:22 - childbirth), (also skin diseases, mildew, bodily ailments)
   Lev. 16:23, 26: The Great Atonement Offering (Lev. 17) Sacredness of blood (John 3:29; I John 1:7).
   Num. 28:9; 28:11: The Sabbath day offering; the first day of the month offering.
   Num. 28:16: Offerings on Major Festivals: Passover, New Year's, Harvest, Atonement, and Festival of the Shelters (ingathering).
   Num. 7: Offerings of leaders.
   Ex. 36:3: Freewill offerings (over and above the rest of the offerings).

3) In review of the offerings and innumerable sacrifices, consider the impact of the Book of Hebrews, particularly chapters 4 and 5: Jesus the Great High Priest; Hebrews 7,8,9, & 10: Christ, the fulfillment of all sacrifices.

4) The Holiness and Justice laws: Lev. 19:25; 8:55.
   Be holy - I Pet. 1:16;
   Be fair -
      a) to poor people.
      b) to foreigners.

5) Aberrations in sexual relationships: Lev. 18; compare Romans 1:26 and I Cor. 6:9 and verses following.

****

BIBLE READING GUIDE
for BIBLE READING PEOPLE

May 1 - Candlesticks and curtains - a   Ex. 27:1-21; 36:8-19
        beautiful place!

2 - Inner veils - outer veils - the   Ex. 36:20-38; 38:1-17
    altar and the court

3 - Overlaid with PURE GOLD   Ex. 38:18-20; 37:25-29;
                                                35:30-35

4 - Dress the Priests in glorious   Ex. 39:1-31
    garments

5 - Take a rest   Ex. 35:1-3

6 - They did as the Lord asked - and   Ex. 39:32-43
    were blessed

7 - No church bells - TRUMPETS CALL   Num. 10:1-10

8 - Get ready for "church"   Ex. 40:1-15

****

REFLECTIONS ON READINGS

May 1 through May 8

Let's get ready for "church".

The readings for this week present the extensive preparations the nation of Israel went through, under God's direction, for the construction of a moving tabernacle which served as their center of worship.

The readings cover the chapters of Ex. 27:1-24; Chapters 36, 37, 38, 39, and 40, and Num. 40:1-15, where the people are called together in various formations for varying occasions.

-20-

In connection with those readings, consider the following:

1) Compare today's church, "Body of Christ", and its relation to God with the relationship of the Israelites and the Covenant of God in the Old Testament, e.g.

   a) Are we more, or less, aware of the presence of God in our lives? Why or why not?

   b) Who are the true Israelites today?
      (1) The Jews living in Palestine?
      (2) The Jews living in the United States?
      (3) The Jews living behind the Iron Curtain in Russia?
      (4) All the people who belong to any Christian denomination?
      (5) All Lutherans, especially LCMS?
      (6) All people who are believers in Jesus Christ?

2) If we could (and would) effectively practice tithing in today's church, how much difference would it make?
      Could we, too, have an "over-offering" (Ex. 36:5)?
      What would we do with the excess?

3) As you have read about the resplendent way in which the Tabernacle Tent was adorned and the way the priests were robed, would you say that today's churches are too luxurious? Not resplendent enough?

   How would you respond to the comment that "We spend too much on buildings; we ought to give that money to the poor"? Or, to missions?

****

May 9 – The Priesthood and the first-born   Num. 3:5-26

    10 – The Priests have to work? Yes,   Num. 3:27-39
         they do!

    11 – Special preparations for the Priests   Num. 3:40-51; 8:5-26

    12 – Various offices and duties of the   Num. 4:16-20; 4:1-15; 4:21-28
         priests

    13 – More duties and responsibilities   Num. 4:29-49
         assigned

    14 – The preparations completed and the   Ex. 40:16:33; Num. 8:1-4;
         Presence of God   Ex. 40:34-35

    15 – The offerings pour in   Num. 7:1-47

****

REFLECTIONS ON READINGS

May 9 through May 15

The priests have work to do? - Yes, they do!

The relation of the first-born and the Levites plus the Aaronitic priesthood: Numbers 3:5-51.

    Special preparation for the priests: Num. 8:5-26.
    The duties and responsibilities of the priests: Num. 4.
    The unique presence of God: Ex. 40:34-35.
    The abundance of offerings for the work of the Lord: Num. 7.

****

May 16 - Just can't give enough to the Lord   Num. 7:48-89

    17 - The annointing and consecration   Num. 3:1-3; Lev. 7:35-36;
         before the congregation   Lev. 8:1-36

    18 - The true and the honest   Lev. 9:1-24

    19 - The false and the fake   Lev. 10:1-7; Num. 3:4

    20 - ATONEMENT DAY   Lev. 16:1-34

    21 - Why sacrifices of blood?   Lev. 17:1-16; 7:37-38; 1:1-17

    22 - The MEAT offering   Lev. 6:8-13; 2:1-16

****

REFLECTIONS ON READINGS

May 16 through May 22

The annointing and consecration of the priests in front of the congregation:
Lev. 7:35-36; Lev. 8:1-36.

Review the "Ordination Rite" and "Installation" of a pastor from the
Lutheran Agenda or service book. Discuss the importance of these rites to our
recognition of the significance of the pastoral office today.

The problem of determining between the false and the fake priests: Lev. 9
and 10.

Consider the details of the GREAT DAY OF ATONEMENT: Lev. 16. Compare Heb. 10,
especially vs. 12 and vs. 19.

Consider the continuing sacrifies: Lev. 1:1-17; 2:1-16; 6:8-23; 7:37-38; and
17:1-16.

****

May 23 - The PEACE offering, WAVE offering   Lev. 3:1-17; 7:11-34
         and the HEAVE offering

     24 - The SIN offering   Lev. 4:1-35; 6:24-30

     25 - The TRESPASS offering   Lev. 5:1-19

     26 - Sin and Trespass offering: FOOD   Lev. 6:1-7; 7:1-10; 10:8-20
          for the priests

     27 - Clean and unclean: What can we eat?   Lev. 11:1-47; 12:1-8

     28 - Sickness and treatment   Lev. 13:1-59

     29 - Lepers and cleansing   Lev. 14:1-57

****

REFLECTIONS ON READINGS

May 23 through May 29

Sacrifices continued: The Peace Offering   Lev. 3:1-17; 7:11-34
                         The Sin Offering   Lev. 4:1-35; 6:24-30
                         The Trespass Offering   Lev. 5:1-19
                         Sin & Trespass Offering   Lev. 6:1-7; 7:1-10; 10:8-20
                         (Food for the Priests)
                         Clean and unclean   Lev. 11:1-47; 12:1-8
                         (What can we eat?)
                         Treating the sick and   Lev. 13:1-59; 14:1-57
                         the lepers

****

May 30 - Rules for cleansing   Lev. 15:1-33

     31 - Nakedness and morality   Lev. 18:1-30; 30; 20:1-6, vs.27

June 1 - Feast days, holidays, celebrations   Lev. 23:1-32

     2 - The Feast of Tabernacles and how   Lev. 23:33-44; 19:1-37
         to behave

     3 - Instructions and qualifications   Lev. 20:7:26; 21:1-24
         of the priests

     4 - Separations, sacrifices, and sins   Lev. 22:1-33; 24:10-23
         of blasphemy

     5 - Murder and camp laws defined   Num. 5:1-31

****

REFLECTIONS ON READINGS

May 30 through June 5

Sexual practices and the cleansing thereof: Lev. 15:1-33; 18:1-30; 20:10-26.

Discuss cultic practices today in the light of Lev. 20:1-6, and vs. 27.

The Great Religious Festivals of Worship in the Old Testament community of believers:

The <u>Passover</u>:	Lev. 23:1-14 (compare Ex. 12 and Num. 28: 16-25; also Num. 9:1-2-23)
The <u>Harvest</u> Festival:	Lev. 23:15-22; (compare Ex. 23:14-19 and Numb. 28:26-31)
The Festival of <u>Shelters</u>:	Lev. 23 33-34; (compare Num. 29:12-40
The <u>New</u> <u>Year</u> Festival:	Lev. 23:23-24; (also called the Festival of <u>Trumpets</u>); compare Num. 29:1-6
The Great Festival of ATONEMENT	Lev. 23:26-27; (compare Lev. 16 and Num. 29:7-11

The high qualifications of the priesthood: Lev. 21, 22.

Discuss capital punishment in the light of Lev. 24:10-22.

****

June	6 - Vows of Nazarites and keeping the Passover	Num. 6:1-27; 9:1-14
	7 - Be sure to count them all	Num. 1:1-54
	8 - Orders of division	Num. 2:1-2; 32-34; 3:1-4
	9 - Let's get on the road	Ex. 33:1-6; Deut. 1:6-18; Num. 10:11-36
	10 - Miraculous leading; does it happen today?	Ex. 40:36-38;　Num. 9:15-23
	11 - Murmuring, complaining; Elders to do the job	Num. 11:1-34
	12 - Problems on the journey	Num. 11:35; 33:17; 12:1-15; 33:18-36

****

June 6 through June 12

Camp laws and sundry matters:	Num. 5.
suspicions of adultery:	Num. 5:11ff.

Rules for the Nazarrite:	Num. 6:1-27.

Census taking is nothing new:	Num. Num. 1.
Orders and divions:	Num. 2.
One tribe for the priesthood:	Num. 3 and Num.26

Let's get on the road: Ex. 33:1-6; Num. 10:11-28; Deut. 1:6-18.

The miraculous leading of the Lord: Ex. 40:36-38; Num. 9:15-23.

Complaints and grievances; settled by the chosen leaders: Num. 11:1-30.

Problems and tribulations among God's people: Num. 12:1-15; Num. 11:31-34.

****

June 13 - Spies and a frightening future	Num. 13:1-24; Deut. 1:21-24 Num. 13:25-33
14 - Why can't you believe?	Deut. 1:25-33; Num. 14:1-24
15 - Cursed to die	Num. 14:25-38; Deut. 1:34-40; Num. 14:36-45
16 - Praises to the Lord most high	Ps. 90 (earliest Psalm); Num. 16:1-22
17 - The seriousness of the Sabbath	Num. 15:37-41; 15:32-36; 16:1-22
18 - God's anger boils over	Num. 16:23-50
19 - Special signs for special significance	Num. 17:1-13

****

REFLECTIONS ON READINGS

June 13 through June 19

Spies discover a frightening future: Num. 13:1-23; Deut. 1:22-33.

Don't be afaid; Why can't you believe? Num. 14:1-46.

In the midst of a struggle, praise the Most High God!: Ps. 90, the earliest Psalm, a Psalm of Moses.

How important the offering: Num. 15:1-31.
How important the Sabbath: Num. 15:32-41. (Compare I. Chron. 6:49; 23:13.

Rebellion among God's people and God's subsequent anger: Num. 15.

Peculiar signs of the significant authority of God: Numbers 17.
A significant question: Discuss how and in what ways do we find rebellion in the midst of God's people today? How and in what ways do we handle it?

****

June 20 - The priests do their duty   Num. 18:1-32

    21 - Strange offerings   Num. 19:1-22

    22 - Trouble with the water supply   Num. 20:1-13; I Chron. 23:16-17

    23 - The death of a leader   Num. 20:14-22; 33:37; 20:23-28;
                                          Num. 33:38-39;Deut. 10:6-7;
                                          Num. 20:29

    24 - Victories along the way   Num. 33:40; 21:1-3;
                                          Deut. 2:1-12
                                          Num. 21:4; 33:41-42

    25 - Sinning and serpents   Num. 21:5-9; 33:43-44;
        (John 3:14-16)   21:10-18; Num. 33:45

    26 - Battles and victories   Num. 33:46-47; 21:19-32

****

REFLECTIONS ON READINGS

June 20 through June 26

The Holy responsibilities of the Priesthood: Num. 18 (note the "Tithe of the Tithe", vs. 25-32).

A strange kind of offering...a red cow: Num. 19.

Trouble with the water supply: Num. 20.
And God's harsh judgement on Moses: Num. 20:12.

The death of leaders of God's people:
    <u>Miriam</u> - Num. 20:1
    <u>Aaron</u>   - Num. 20:24ff; 33:38-39; Lev. 10:6-7.

Significant victories on the way to the Promised Land: Num. 21:1-4;
Lev. 2:1-12; Num. 21:10-35.

For <u>sharing</u>: Discuss your personal victories of faith as you travel to the
               Promised Land.

The crucified serpent becomes the prototype of the crucified Savior. Compare
Num. 21:49 with John 3:14-17.

****

June 27 - Taking the cities in stride	Deut. 2:19-37	
28 - Victories over powerful Kings	Deut. 3:1-11; Num. 21:33-35; Num. 22:1; 33:48-49	
29 - When God gets angry, strange things can happen	Num. 22:2-41	
30 - Prophetic voices	Num. 23:1-30	
July 1 - Vision from the Almighty	Num. 24:1-25; 25:1-18	
2 - Another Census	Num. 26:1-65	
3 - Women's rights to inheritance	Num. 27:1-11; 28:1-31	

****

<u>REFLECTIONS ON READINGS</u>

June 27 through July 3

Cities and kings succumb to the power and advance of God's people:
Deut. 2:16-37; 3:1-11.

God's anger created strange scenes (commonly known as the story of Balaam's
stubborn donkey): Num. 22:2-41.

Three significant prophesies concerning the nation of Israel: Num. 23 & 24.
Look for them and discuss their meanings.

A good Law/Gospel message: <u>Judgement</u> and <u>forgiveness</u> - Num. 25.

Concerning women's rights: Num. 27:1-11

****

BIBLE READING GUIDE
for BIBLE READING PEOPLE

July 4 – Trumpets and Tabernacles   Num. 29:1-40

       5 – Holy Wars   Num. 30:1-16; 31:1-54

       6 – Settlement claims of conquered   Num. 32:1-42
           lands

       7 – Territorial claims; NO territory   Deut. 3:12-17; Joshua 13:8-32
           for the Priests BUT

       8 – Recall the victories: Prepare   Jos. 12:1-6; Num. 33:50-56;
           for conquest   Deut. 3:18-29

       9 – Dividing the spoils   Num. 34:1-29

      10 – Even the criminal needs some   Num. 35:1-34
           protection

****

REFLECTIONS ON READINGS

July 4 through July 10

Sounding off to God's Glory; Trumpets and Tabernacles: Num. 29:1-40.

When you get married, MEAN IT!: Num. 30.

Off to the Holy Wars: Num. 31
  settlement claims: Num. 32; 33:50-56
  the Lord will fight for you: Deut. 3:12-29; Jos. 12:1-6
  dividing the spoils: Num. 34

Cities of refuge: Protection even for the criminal: Num.35;
                                                      Deut. 4:41-49
                                                      Deut. 19:1-13

****

July 11 – Detailed instructions; Cities   Deut. 4:41-49; 19:1-13
           of Refuge

       12 – Laws to be remembered   Num. 36:1-12; Deut. 1:1-5;
                                                      Duet. 4:1-40

       13 – Remember Sinai   Deut. 5:1-33

       14 – The First and Great Commandment   Deut. 6:1-25

       15 – You belong to the Lord; count it   Deut. 7:1-26
            a blessing!

July 16 – Promise of the Good Land   Deut. 8:1-20

    17 – Disgusting Disobedience   Deut. 9:1-29

****

REFLECTIONS ON READING

July 11 through July 17

Military and civilians, all in the census: Num. 26.

Remember Mt. Sinai: Deut. 1:1-5; 4:1-40; 5:1-33.

The greatest commandment: Deut. 6:1-25.
                    Compare Matt. 22:34-39; Mark 12:28-34; Luke 10:25-28

You are God's people. Why?
                  Because He loved you, that's why! Deut. 7:1-26.
                  Compare I John 4:7-10.

The promised possession; live in the promise: Deut. 8:1-20.

Disgusting disobedience: Deut. 9:1-29.
                  Compare Deut. 9:9 with Luke 4:1-13

****

July 18 – The Commandments and the Covenant   Deut. 10:1-22

    19 – The Blessings are all yours, IF   Deut. 11:1-32

    20 – One God, one place to Worship   Deut. 12:1-32

    21 – Watch out for the false prophets   Deut. 13:1-18

    22 – Tithes and Tithes of Tithe   Deut. 14:1-29

    23 – The seventh year release   Deut. 15:1-23
        (Sabbatic Year)

    24 – Remember the Passover   Deut. 16:1-22

****

July 18 through July 24

God's promises and ours: Deut. 10:1-22.

The blessings are ours, IF: Deut. 11:1-32.

God gets specific and <u>our</u> worship: Deut. 12:1-32.

Testing for false prophets: Deut. 13:1-18. Compare I John 4:1-6.

Tithing for all and Tithes of the Tithes (Levites): Deut. 14:1-29.

Sabbatical years...cancel everything: Deut. 15:1-23.

The Great Festivals (Passover, Harvest, Shelters) remember: Deut. 15:1-23.

****

July 25 - Justices, Judges, and Kings	Deut. 17:1-20
26 - Of Priests, pagans and prophets	Deut. 18:1-22
27 - Tell the whole truth and nothing but the <u>whole</u> <u>truth</u>	Deut. 19:14-21
118 - The nerve to fight; an ingredient of war	Deut. 20:1-20
29 - Laws for contingencies	Deut. 21:1-23
30 - Duties in disputes	Deut. 25:1-19
31 - Sex, Sacred or Sensual?	Deut. 22:1-30

****

REFLECTIONS ON READINGS

July 25 through July 31

Justice and Judges and Kings: Deut. 17:1-20.

Priests and Pagans and Prophets: Deut. 18:1-22.

The truth, the whole truth and nothing but the truth: Deut. 19:14-21.

Contingency Laws: Deut. 21:1-23
    Duties in disputes   Deut. 25:1-19
    Sex, Sacred & Sensual   Deut. 22:1-30

****

BIBLE READING GUIDE
for BIBLE READING PEOPLE

August 1 - Keep the camp clean   Deut. 23:1-25

        2 - Laws of divorce and remarriage   Deut. 24:1-22

        3 - Giving and praying   Deut. 26:1-19; 27:1-26

        4 - Blessings proportional to   Deut. 28:1-40
            obedience to God

        5 - Disobedience leads to the   Deut. 28:41-68

        6 - The promise in the presence   Deut. 29:1-29
            of the Lord

        7 - A new officer in charge   Deut. 30:1-20;
            Num. 36:12; Num. 27:15-23

****

REFLECTIONS ON READINGS

August 1 through August 7

Deuteronomy Review:
Deuteronomy is a concise summary and review of what happened to Israel from
the time of the Exodus (1492 B.C.) up to the time of their entrance (perman-
ently) into the Land of Canaan (1422 B.C.).

The key of Deuteronomy is Chapter 6:4-9, 11:18ff, prompting us to ask:
"How fervently do we conduct religious and spiritual activities in our
homes?"

Various and sundry laws for the guidance of God's people: Deut. 23:1-25.
        Exclusions from the fellowship: vs. 1-8.
        Keep the camp clean: vs. 9-14.
        Concerning slaves and prostitutes: vs. 15-17.
        Concerning lending for interest: vs. 19-20.
        KEEP YOUR PROMISES TO GOD: vs. 21-25.

A good time to review your baptismal and confirmation vows.

Laws of divorce and remarriage: Deut. 24:1-4.

For contemporary viewing of the challenge of marriage and the problem of
divorce, consider and discuss the following:

        THE MAJOR MARRIAGE PRINCIPLE: Genesis 2:18-24.
                Are there exceptions? - Mark 10:1-11; Matt. 19:1-12; I Cor. 7:1-39;
                                Luke 16:18; Matt. 5:31ff.

        What are the exceptions? - Matt. 19:9; I Cor. 7:13-15

What is the church's role in relating to marital problems, separation, and divorce? Rate the following statements on a scale of 1 to 10.

_____ to reassert the principle of "Til death do us part"?

_____ to pronounce judgement for the wrong?

_____ to pronounce judgement with attending condemnation?

_____ to refuse communion unless there is a reconciliation?

_____ to excommunicate both parties?

_____ to determine who is the innocent party and excommunicate the guilty party?

_____ to lead and counsel in confession and pronounce absolution?

_____ to keep hands off; don't interfere?

_____ to pronounce forgiveness and help people pick up the pieces and proceed with life, making the best of the circumstances?

_____ to give continued blessing, counsel, and follow-up sharing the love of Christ?

Any other options:

On giving and praying: Deut. 26:1-19; 27:1-26.

Blessings of obedience: Deut. 28:1-68.

The Lord's promise and our response: Deut. 29:1-29.

Take your choice: A BLESSING or A CURSE...between LIFE or DEATH:
Deut. 30:1-20; Num. 36:13.

****

August 8 - The farewell message of Moses   Deut. 31:1-13; 31:23-29

        9 - God's final instruction to His   Deut. 3L;14-22
            Chosen Leader

       10 - The swan song of the Captain of   Deut. 31:30; 32:1-47
            Israel

August 11 – Just you and me, God; and the   Num. 27:12-14;
            people that you gave me   Deut. 32:48-52; 33:1-29

       12 – Death and a new beginning   Ps. 91:1-16;
                                                   Deut. 34:1-12

       13 – The sum of history in Psalms   Ps. 78:12-66

       14 – The sume of history in Psalms   Ps. 105:16-45; 106:1-33

****

REFLECTIONS ON READINGS

August 8 through August 14

The "Swan Song" of the faithful leader, Moses: Deut. 31, 32, 33, and 34.

Psalms, presumably authored by Moses, are read in connection with this period.
    (e.g., Ps. 90 – The earliest Psalm)

Of death and a new beginning: Ps. 91.

The sum of history in Psalms: Ps. 78, 105, 106; Review I Chron. 16:8-22;
                               Ps. 135.

****

August 15 – The sum of history in Psalms   Ps. 135:1-21

       16 – General heading for the readings   Joshua 1:1-9; 3:1; 2:1-21
            that follow: FROM THE CROSSING
            INTO CANAAN TO THE REIGN OF KING SAUL (1422-1065 B.C.)

       17 – Look for the wonders of the Lord   Josh. 2:22-24; 1:10-18; 3:2-13

       18 – A wide, wide river to cross   Josh. 3:14-17; 4:1-18

       19 – The memory of God's message   Ps. 114:18; Josh. 4:19-24;
            moves a memorial to His might   Josh. 5:1-9

       20 – Invasion and conquest   Josh. 5:10-12; 6:11; 5:13-15;
                                                   Josh. 6:2-20

       21 – No cover-up with God   Josh. 6:21-27; 7:1-26

****

REFLECTIONS ON READINGS

August 15 through August 21

A new leader, Joshua, for a new time: Numbers 27:12-23

A wide, wide river to cross: Joshua 1, 2, and 3

Discuss the practice of Memorials that we exercise today. Recount and remember the Memorials given in your congregation. Do you remember the names of those in whose memory the gifts were given?

Invasion and Conquests:
     Circumcision Hill   Joshua 5:12
     A Commander of the Lord's Army   "   5:13-35
     A strange assault strategy   "   6
     A set-back to the attack   "   7
     Back on the road to victory   "   8

****

August 22 - Back on victory road   Joshua 8:1-29

    23 - When God has blessed --   Joshua 8:30-35; 9:1-27
         build an altar

    24 - A special angel with a   Judges 2:1-5
         special message

    25 - The longest day in history   Joshua 10:1-27

    26 - The Lord delivers - Again and again Joshua 10:28-43

    27 - The total conquest and a time   Joshua 11:1-23

    28 - The review of the conquest   Joshua 12:7-24; 13:1-6

****

REFLECTIONS ON READINGS

August 22 through August 28

BUILDING ALTARS -- A good response: Joshua 8:30-35

Days of deception: "   9:1-27

And what did the angel say?   Judges 2:1-5

When the sun stands still--It's a long day: Joshua 10

After the victory -- time to rest: "   11

A review of the conquest by
Moses and Joshua: "   12

August 29 - Dividing the spoils of war   Joshua 13:7; 14:1-15

      30 - Further division for the   Joshua 15:13-19; Judges 1:20
         conquerors   1:10-16; I Chronicles 6:56

      31 - Drawing up the borderlines of   Joshua 15:1-12; 15:20-63;
         of the new lands   Judges 1:21

Sept.   1 - Territorial troubles   Joshua 16:1-10; 17:1-18

       2 - A Tabernacle in a Tent --   Joshua 18:1-28

       3 - Portions for the people   Joshua 19:1-31
         of the tribe   I Chronicles 4:28-33

       4 - Portions for prisoners   Joshua 19:32-51; 20:1-9

****

REFLECTIONS ON READINGS

August 29 through September 4

To the winners -- the spoils: -- Joshua 13 & 14; Judges 1:10-20; I Chron.6:56

Drawing up the borderlines of the new lands --   Joshua 15; 16; & 17

What a beautiful "tent" for worship!   --------   Joshua 18

Portions for the people   -----   Joshua 19; I Chronicles 4:28-31

The prisoners refuge ---------   Joshua 20: 1-9

Reflect on all the above and on contemporary modes of dealing with prisoners

****

Sept. 5 - Portions for priests   Joshua 13:14; 13:33; 21:1-42

      6 - Cities and suburbs   I Chronicles 6:54-81

      7 - Homes over the Jordan   Joshua 22:1-34

      8 - The Lord and the judges   Judges 3:5-10

      9 - Joshua's last call   Joshua 23:1-16

    10 - A TIME FOR DECISION   Joshua 24:1-28

****

September 5 through September 10

The priests of God are not forgotten -- Joshua 13:14; 13:33; 21:1-42
   Discuss: Do we, as Christians today, adequately provide for the
            called ministers of our parish? How and in what way?

            Discuss the pros and cons of a pastor owning his own home
            or being provided a parsonage by the congregation.
            Are there other alternatives?

            What is the salary of the servant(s) of God in your parish?
            Do you think it is adeauate? How may the needs of pastors vary?

A furor over where to build the church?

            How important is the altar and worship center in the lives
            of Christians today? Discuss Joshua 22.

Study the impact of Joshua's farewell message to his people --Joshua 23 and 24

            Compare Paul's farewell to the congregation at Ephesus.
            Acts 20:17ff

****

Sept. 11 - Burials--Joshua -Joseph -- The end of an era	Judges 2:6-7; Joshua 24:29-31 Judges 2:8-9
12 - The beginning of the backslide - A time to beware	Judges 1:22-36; 2:10-23
13 - Perplexity and peace	Judges 3:1-4; 11-14; Joshua 24:33; Judges 3:15-30
14 - No king in Israel	Judges 17:1-13; 18:1-31
15 - Sexual perversion is nothing new	Judges 19:1-30
16 - CIVIL WAR (1325 B.C.)	Judges 20:1-48
17 - No king --Everyone did what he (or she) pleased!	Judges 21:1-25
18 - Twenty years of oppression	Judges 3:31; 4:1-3

****

REFLECTIONS ON READINGS

September 11 through September 18

REFLECTION ON JUDGES: The last verse of the last chapter of Judges reflects the

<u>tumultous situation</u> of the time between the leadership of Moses and Joshua and the coming of the kings: Saul, David, and Solomon. It represents a time frame of 410 years (?)- Some say as little a 150 years: (Deborah - 50) Gideon - 50) (Jotham - 50). Othniel, Ehud, Shamgar, Abimelech, Tulah, Jair and Jephthah are then considered tribal administrators, as well as military leaders.

Questions for reflection:

   1 - Where did the judges come from? Exodus 18:12ff; Deuteronomy 1:9ff.

   2 - Discuss the whole concept of testing. Judges 3:1-3; 6:13-32
       Have you in a personal way ever put God to the test? In what way do you think God may have laid tests on America as a nation? Any other nations? Upon you as an individual?

   3 - Chapters 17 - 20 are replete with problems:
       a - The power of conscience (17:1-5)
       b - Deception and thievery (18:7ff)
       c - Priestly perversion: sacrificing integrity for security (18:19)
       d - The power syndrome: "Might makes Right" (18:25)
       e - Transient problems (19:15ff)
       f - Sexual perversion (vs.22)
       g - The whole problem of war (Chapter 20)

****

Sept. 19 - The beginning of a beautiful   Ruth 1:1-22
            romance

   20 - The man's name is Boaz   Ruth 2:1-23

   21 - Love grows   Ruth 3:1-18

   22 - Married-The ultimate of human love   Ruth 4:4-24

   23 - A prophetess--What?   Judges 4:4-24
         A woman judge?

   24 - And a musician, too!   Judges 5:1-31

****

<u>REFLECTIONS ON READINGS</u>

September 19 through September 24

Discuss: Dedicated family loyalty as found in the beautiful story of Ruth.
      Consider the problems of loneliness that develop through the loss of a
      loved one. (Ruth 1:1-5) How best to share and strengthen?

A great example of devotion between mother and daughter-in-law:(Ruth 1-22)

The courting of Ruth and Boaz: (Ruth 3 & 4)
      Reflect on how you met your spouse --
      How did your love develop? What makes love grow?

What prominence did the blessing of God (vs.20) have in your meeting and in your marriage?

Does the Lord receive the praise for the blessing of your children and their children in your progeny?

The Role of women in Israelite history:

Deborah, Prophet and Judge (Judges 4)
Women warriors (Judges 9:53)

How would you assess the current situation of women in politics?
Women in the military?
A woman singer in the community of saints?

****

Sept. 25 -	Backsliding again!	Judges 6:1-10
26 -	Why does God permit all this evil? (verse 13)	Judges 6:11-40
27 -	God doesn't need all this man-power	Judges 7:1-25
28 -	A final victory -- Peace and death	Judges 8:1-35
29 -	A violent end to a short reign	Judges 9:1-57
30 -	The prophecy and prediction of a powerful man	Judges 10:1-5; 13:2-25
October 1 -	The feeling of being forlorn	Judges 11:1-3; I Samuel 1:1-28
2 -	Songs of deliverance -- Sins of apostasy	Judges 13:1; Psalm 106:34-46

****

REFLECTIONS ON READINGS

September 25 through October 2

Back to the ways of backsliding again! (Judges 6:1-10)

Discuss: The problems of backsliding in the church

The problems of evil in the world (Judges 6:11-40)
Whose fault is it? Vs. 13)

Have you ever used a "fleece" to determine the will of God in your life? Share your experience.

How much manpower does God need to fight a war? (Judges 7:1-25)

Trial and trouble between the tribes and the leaders of God's people - Judges 8
    The short-sightedness of leaders and people
    How do we show gratitude for the faithfulness of good leaders in our
    church and nation?

A violent and short reign - Joshua 9:1-57
    Politics and power don't always produce peace - vs. 22-24

The prophecy and prediction of a powerful man
    His birth - Joshua 13:2-25
    Discuss dedication of children to God. Are we as sensitive to purpose - Vs.12

Discuss the frustration of feeling rejected and forlorn as in the case of
    Hannah - I Samuel 1:1-28

the joy of deliverance - I Samuel 2; Psalm 106:34-46

How and in what ways has God answered special prayers that have brought joy to
    your life?

****

October 3 - Faithlessness in God's families   Judges 14:1-20; 15:1-2
                                                    I Samuel 2:11-17

        4 - Faithless son of the servants   I Samuel 2:18-36
            in God's family

        5 - A faithful servant in God's   I Samuel 3:1-21
            family

        6 - Another time for wars and   Judges 11:4-40
            warriors

        7 - Shibbuleth or Sibboleth -   Judges 12:1-7; 15-20
            clear speach is important!

        8 - Ichabod - the glory departs   I Samuel 4:1-22: 5:1-12
            from Israel

        9 - Don't fool with the Ark of   I Samuel 6:1-21; 7:1-2
            the Lord

****

REFLECTIONS ON READINGS

October 3 through October 9

A beloved son begins his service to the Lord: I Samuel 2:11; 2:18-21; 2:26
        Compare Luke 2:39-52
        Discuss what prompts young men (or women) to go into the ministry today?
        Ask your pastor how he got into the full-time service of the church.
        Ask other church workers as well.

Troubles in the household of the priest of God: I Samuel 2:22-36
    Discuss the special problems and privileges that may go with being in the
    pastor's family today.

A special call of the Lord to a special person: I Samuel 3:1-21

Discuss the personal relationship involved as the people search for a leader
    Judges 11:1-40
    What do you think may have been the deeper problems in the relationship
    of Jephtha and his daughter

An interesting sidelight. The importance of our accent betraying our "bringing
    up" and where we are from: Judges 12:1-13

A sad day of war and its traumatic consequences: I Samuel 4 & 5
    Discuss the impact of verse 22 - Ichabod. Are there times when a country
    or a church or a congregation may experience that in modern times?

Renew your memory of the Covenant Box: I Samuel 6:1-21; 7:1-2
    Where did it come from: Exodus 25:10 ff; 37:1-9
    What it contained: Exodus 26:33ff
    Discuss the concept of <u>covenant.</u>

Discuss the difference represented in the concepts of Ichabod (I Samuel 4:22)
    and Ebenezer: I Samuel 7:12

Check out the original experience at Mizpah: Genesis 31:49

An exchange of vengeance and violence: Judges 15:3-20

****

October 10 - A revolutionary in the ranks	Judges 12:8-10; 15:3-19; 16:1-3; I Samuel 14:49-50
11 - Deceptive Delilah	Judges 12:11-12; 16:4-31
12 - Revival and rejuvenation	I Samuel 7:3-17; Judges 12:13-15 I Samuel 8:1-22
13 - The beginning of the kings	I Samuel 9:1-27
14 - The anointing and inauguration of Israel's first king	I Samuel 10:1-27
15 - The people celebrate with peace offerings	I Samuel 11:1-15; I Chronicles 5:10-22
16 - Samuel the prophet speaks to the people	I Samuel 12:1-25

October 10 through October 16

REFLECTION ON SAMUEL: The book of Samuel is abundant with lessons of application to everyday life. It covers everything from feuding families to feuding females:

        Chapter 1 - Beautiful answers to prayer
                2 - The joys of motherhood
                3 - Rebellious sons
                4 - Prophecies and fulfillment through dreams and revelations (2-3)
                5 - Disruptions and unfaithfulness in the midst of God's people
                6 - Ichabod - God's glory gone (4:22)

Problems of demons and control by evil spirits (19) -divinations: (I Samuel: 28)

Characteristics of God puzzling to man: (Psalm 11)
        Psalms of imprecation -- (Does God really hate?)
        Is it justifiable for us to hate sin and sinners? (Psalm 11)

The problems of secular government and sacred obligations: (I Timothy 4:14-15;
        I Samuel 4 & 8)

The mixed emotions of faith, fear and frustration: (Psalm 26; I Samuel 21)

Prayers - Praise - Promises: (Psalm 34 & 56) -- Compare Romans 8:18-37

Severe injustices and massacres by men in power: (22:6-20)

Studies in human dynamics: (I Samuel 18; 25; & 26)
        Problems of vengeance:(I Samuel 14)
        God's vengeance and our vengeance--There is a difference: (Romans 12:19)
        Woman's place in a man's world: (I Samuel 25)

Three ways God speaks: (I Samuel 28:5)

****

October 17 - Saul, the King; Samuel, the   I Samuel 13:1-23
             servant - CLASH

        18 - The Lord can win, no matter   I Samuel 14:1-46
             what the size of the army

        19 - Saul slips into sin   I Samuel 14:47-52; 15:1-35

        20 - The rise and the fall of kings   I Samuel 16:1-11; Psalm 39:1-13
                                                  I Samuel 16:12-13; Psalm 19:1-14

        21 - Soothing music refreshes the   Psalm 8:1-9; I Samuel 16:14-23;
             soul   17:1-54

        22 - Beset by fear-Delivered by faith   I Samuel 17:5-54; 18:1-4

        23 - A Psalm of confidence in God   Psalm 23

October 17 through October 23

Consider and discuss this contemporary paraphrase of Psalm 23:

> The Lord is my security.
>   He fills all my need.
>   He is my carpeted floor
>   and the foam rubber in my mattress.
> He keeps the water running in my air conditioner - and
>   keeps me cool.
> He strengthens and forgives me when I feel guilty
>   and tells me how to live right,
>   that in his mercy I may magnify Him!
> Even tho' I know that I am going to die,
>   I am not afraid.
> For He is with me, even in death.
> Even when He disciplines and directs me, I feel safe.
> When the going is tough because people pick on me,
>   He gives me big meals.
> He massages my brow when I am worried.
>   I have more than I can drink.
> How good God is, and I know He is going
>   to bless me with His steadfast love,
>   as long as I live in this old world,
>   and when that's over, I'm going to have the
>   biggest and best house yet - Because it's God's house,
>   and I'm going to live in it forever.

(LEW)

BIBLE READING GUIDE
for BIBLE READING PEOPLE

October 24 -	Being popular has its rank and RISK	I Samuel 18:5-13; Psalm 5:1-12 I Samuel 18:14-19
25 -	Marrying the king's daughter can be dangerous	I Samuel 18:20-30; Psalm 12:1-8
26 -	A man with emotional problems	Psalm 11:1-7; I Samuel 19:1-3
27 -	A servant of the Lord has to flee for life	Psalm 59:1-17; I Samuel 19:4-24 Psalm 7:1-17
28 -	A prayer of hopeful trust in a time of danger	Psalm 25:1-22
29 -	A faithful friend loves as a brother	I Samuel 20:1-42
30 -	Faith, fear, and frustration - Mixed emotions of a man of God	Psalm 26:1-12; I Samuel 21:1-15
31 -	Songs of praise, prayer. and promises	Psalm 34:1-22; 56:1-13

REFLECTIONS ON READINGS

October 24 through October 31

How much jealousy between individuals and organizations influence our political leaders? Church organizations. congregations and denominations?

Do you think a psychiatrist would have been able to help Saul in his emotional disturbance? (I Samuel 18) Give reasons for your answer.

To what extent do think "evil spirits" are responsible for emotional disturbances in the lives of people today? Discuss I Samuel 19:9

Discuss how pastoral counseling and psychiatrical counseling relate today?

Discuss the friendship of Jonathan and David: (I Samuel 20)
    Define "friend"--What makes a person acceptable as a friend?
    Describe the characteristics of your best friend

Have you ever felt the need of praying a prayer like Psalm 26?

How about the praise Psalms - 34 & 56?

****

BIBLE READING GUIDE
for BIBLE READING PEOPLE

November 1 - Peace in the midst of ponderous problems — I Samuel 22:1-2: I Chronicles 12:16-18: Psalm 142:1-7; Psalm 141:1-10; I Samuel 22:3-5; Psalm 64:1-10

2 - 85 priests sacrificed to injustice by a paranoid king — I Samuel 22:6-20; Psalm 35:1-28;

3 - Stay with me and don't be afraid — I Samuel 23:1-5; 22:21-23; Psalm 52:1-9; 109:1-3

4 - Kept on the move by the advice of God — Psalm 140:1-3; I Samuel 23:6-13; Psalm 31:1-24

5 - A cherished promise of friendship — I Samuel 23:14-15; Psalm 13:1-6; I Samuel 23:16-28; Psalm 54:1-7

6 - "Evil is done only by evil men!" (verse 13) — I Samuel 23:29; Psalm 17:1-15; I Samuel 24:1-22

****

REFLECTIONS ON READINGS

November 1 through November 6

At what times in your life have you felt the protection of "family" - in

what way? - (I Samuel 22:1-2)
        Was it your immediate family? - the church family? - friendship family?
        or other? - (I Chronicles 12:16ff)
        Compare the parable, the Prodigal Son and his family: (Luke 15:11ff)

Study Psalm 142; 141; and 64. Have you used Psalms as these when you were
lonely and in trouble? Did you find them helpful? How and in what ways?

Have you felt the pain of injustice in your life? Share the circumstances if
you can. Apply Psalm 25 to those circumstances. Compare I Samuel 22/

How do you feel God directs your life in painful circumstances? Any relation
to I Samuel 23?

****

BIBLE READING GUIDE
for BIBLE READING PEOPLE

November 7 - Mourning for the servant Saul	Psalm 57:1-11; 108:1-5; I Samuel 25:1
8 - A mean man saved by a merciful woman	I Samuel 25:2-38
9 - Saul saved again by his successor	I Samuel 25:39-44; 26:1-25
10 - Sublety and subservience by sinful men	I Samuel 27:1-12; I Chronicles 12:1-7; I Samuel 28:1-2
11 - The Lord gives courage	I Samuel 29:1-11; I Chronicles 12:19-22; I Samuel 30:1-6
12 - Greedy grouchers have no place in the plan of mercy	I Samuel 30:7-31
13 - Abandoned by God - How terrifying!	I Samuel 28:3-25
14 - A very sad ending for Father Saul and his sons	I Samuel 31:1-13; I Chronicles 10:1-14

****

REFLECTIONS ON READINGS

November 7 through November 14

Discuss Psalm 57 and Psalm 108:1-5, as tools for meditation in times of extreme
difficulty and depression.

Discuss a woman"s place in a man's world on the basis of I Samuel 25, then and now

Is it right to rejoice and praise God for another person's death? Discuss this
according to I Samuel 25:39-43, especially verse 39.
Compare and discuss the imprecatory Psalms 58 and 109.

Discuss the contradiction of I Samuel 25:39 and the circumstances of I Samuel 26 & 27. How do we respond to people who conspire evil against us?

Study the problem of rejection in the light of I Samuel 29. What would you do in a similar situation?

Discuss the attitudes of gratitude as shown by David and some of his followers in I Samuel 30.

What about mediums and spirits and "ouija boards"?

Discuss the attitudes of various people in I Samuel 31. Compare I Chronicles 10.

Discuss the problem of suicide - for Saul. Have you ever experienced a relationship with a person who later committed suicide? What were the problems that led to that person's suicide? What were your thoughts and feelings?

Discuss "Suicide is the ultimate of self-consciousness. Nothing exists for the man but himself, and when this happens there is no reason for him to exist either." Interpreter's Bible, Volume 2, page 1040.

****

BIBLE READING GUIDE
    for BIBLE READING PEOPLE

November 15 - David's lament - brave soldiers   II Samuel 4:4; 1:1-27
                have fallen

         16 - Ancestry and descendants of King   I Chronicles 8:29-40; 9:35-44
                Saul

         17 - The end of fighting - BITTERNESS   II Samuel 5:4; I Kings 2:11;
                                                   I Chron. 29:27; II Samuel 2:1-32

         18 - The trial and troubles of   II Samuel 3:1-5; I Chronicles
                transition   3:1-4; II Samuel 3:6-21

         19 - Criminal murders didn't start   II Samuel 3:22-29
                with our generation

         20 - Through turmoil a king is   II Samuel 4:1-12; 5:1-3;
                crowned   I Chronicles 11:1-2

         21 - The warriors worship   I Chronicles 12:23-40; 29:26;
                                                   II Samuel 5:5; Psalm 58:1-11

****

REFLECTIONS ON READINGS

November 15 through November 21

A Biblical contradiction (I Samuel 1:10 -- II Samuel 4:4): Was Saul a suicide or was he killed by another soldier? Discuss.

Put the question of II Samuel 2:26 into the current dilemma of continuing wars.
    What is your answer?

Discuss the intrigue and deception of men in power according to II Samuel 3 & 4.

****

November 22 - The Psalms and songs for   Psalm 93:1-5; 95:1-11; II Samuel
              coronation   5:6-10; I Chronicles 11:4-9;
                                                Psalm 118: 5-28

        23 - What's a king without a house?!   II Samuel 5:11-16; I Chronicles
                                                14:1-2; Psalm 101:1-8; I Chronicles
                                                3:5-9; & 14:3-7

        24 - Wars in the valley   II Samuel 5:17-18; I Chronicles
                                                14:8-9; & 12:8-15; II Samuel
                                                23:13-17; I Chronicles 13:1-4

        25 - Victories lead to further   II Samuel 5:19-25
             conflict   I Chronicles 14:10-17

        26 - Where, oh where, can I go   Psalm 139:1-24; II Samuel 6:1-5
             to escape from God?   I Chronicles 13:5-8

        27 - Celebrating God's Covenant   Psalm 78:1-11; 78:67-72;
                                                II Samuel 6:6-11

        28 - Praise and preparation in   Psalm 68:1-35;
             God's presence   I Chronicles 15:1-14

        29 - Music and shouting for joy!   Psalm 132:1-18;
                                                I Chronicles 15:15-24

        30 - Singing and dancing to the   II Samuel 6:12-17; I Chronicles
             glory of God   15:25-29; Psalm 97:1-42;
                                                II Chronicles 1:4; Psalm 15:1-5

****

REFLECTIONS ON READINGS

November 22 through November 30

"Once in royal David's City"

    Discuss the difference of circumstances of David's City as in II Samuel 5:9
    with David's City at the time of the birth of Christ. I Chron. 11:5; Luke 2:4

    Consider and discuss the Royalty Psalms: 93; 95; 118; 101. How do we
    reflect recognition of divine rule in our inaugural celebrations?

Reflect on God's direct messages and instructions to David - II Samuel 5:17ff.
How does God speak to His people today? How does He speak to YOU?

Discuss nations in conflict: I Chronicles 14:8-17.
How does God show His presence in battles today?

Remembering the Covenant Box: I Chronicles 13.

Reflect on its meaning.
What about God's promises? Psalm 139:78.
To Israel and to us?
Discuss II Samuel 6:1-23

Share the joy of Psalms 68; 132; 97; and 15.

****

BIBLE READING GUIDE
for BIBLE READING PEOPLE

December 1 - Ministers to serve - to thank -   Psalm 24:1-10; II Samuel 6:18-19;
and to praise the Lord!   I Chronicles 16:1-22; Ps. 105:1-15

2 - Songs - Offerings -   I Chronicles 16:23-43; Psalm 96:
Thanksgiving to God   1-13; Psalm 98:1-9; 106:47-48

3 - Who's going to build the   II Samuel 6:20-23; 7:1-17;
house for the Lord?   I Chronicles 17:1-2

4 - Who am I??   I Chronicles 17:3-15; II Samuel
Let YOUR WORD be so, Oh Lord! 7:18-29; I Chronicles 17:16-27

5 - God's victories are worth   Psalm 2:1-12; 110:1-7; 16:1-11;
shouting about!   II Samuel 8:1-8; I Chron. 18:1-2

6 - God has spoken in His holiness: I Chronicles 18:3-6; Psalm 9:1-20;
I will rejoice!   II Samuel 8:9-11; II Chronicles
                               18:9-10; Psalm 60:1-12

7 - Vain is the help of man   Psalm 108:6-13; II Samuel 8:12-14;
                               I Chronicles 18:11-13; I Kings
                               11;15-20; II Samuel 23:8-39

8 - Chiefs of the mighty men   I Chronicles 11:10-47; II Samuel
                               8:15-18; I Chronicles 18:14-17

****

REFLECTIONS ON READINGS

December 1 through December 8

Who is the King? - Share thoughts on Psalm 24.

Discuss the term "forensic justification" in the light of Psalm 24:5.

Compare Psalm 24 in the light of its messianic content with John 18:33-38
and Rev. 19:11-16.

Discuss the joy of being in "covenant" with God: See II Samuel 6:1-23;
and I Chronicles 16:1-43.

How do our worship services reflect the concept of "covenant"?
Reflect on Psalms 96:98 and 106:47-48 as Psalms of praise.

What is the importance of God's House as a place for worship? And, who is to
build it? I Chronicles 17:1-27 and II Samuel 7:1-29.

Can we be as charitable as David when we discover that God has another way,
rather than "our way"?

Rejoice in victory: II Samuel 8:1-18; I Chronicles 18:1-17.
Reflect on our victory, through Christ, as Psalms 2 and 110 indicate.
Compare Hebrews 7:11-28.

In time of trouble there is still reason for rejoicing: Psalm 9 & Psalm 60.

When compared to the help of God, man's efforts are vain indeed: Psalm 108

****

BIBLE READING GUIDE
    for BIBLE READING PEOPLE

December 9 - A great song of deliverance   II Samuel 22:1-51

        10 - A pledge of loyalty and thanks   Psalm 18:1-50

        11 - A love song carrried into   Psalm 144:1-15; II Samuel 9:1-13

        12 - War games played for keeps --   II Samuel 10:1-14;
             So what's new?   I Chronicles 19:1-15

        13 - Victories and vices -- the   II Samuel 10:15-19; I Chron. 19:
             plagues of God's people   16-19; Psalm 20:1-9; I Kings 15:5;
                                                II Samuel 11:1-27

        14 - Reproof, repentance, and   II Samuel 12:1-15;
             redemption   Psalm 51:1-;9

        15 - Failed -- but forgiven --   Psalm 32:1-11; 38:1-22; 103:1-22
             and good fortune

        16 - Trauma -- sadness because   II Samuel 12:16-25;
             of a child's death   Psalm 6:1-10

December 9 through December 16

A great song of confidence and trust in deliverance: II Samuel 22:1-51.
    Compare this account with any deliverances you have experienced
    in your life. Share.
    Discuss Luther's phrase, "saved me with great cost, from sin, death and
    the power of the devil": (2nd Article - meaning - Catechism) -- in the
    light of that deliverance.

How do we respond? refer again to Luther's explanation -- 2nd Art.
    Also Psalm 18:1-50.

Love in action and praise. Psalm 144: - and sharing. - II Samuel 9:1-13.

War games for keeps -- II Samuel 10:1-14; I Chronicles 19:1-15.
    Compare Luke 21:9. Discuss.

Intrigue and deception for personal gain. Does it pay?
    Consider II Samuel 11:1-27; 12:1-23.

Discuss repentance and redemption in the light of Psalm 51; 52; and 103.

****

BIBLE READING GUIDE
        for BIBLE READING PEOPLE

December 17 -	The powerful emotion of immorality	II Samuel 12:26-31; I Chronicles 20:1-3; Psalm 21:1-13; II Samuel 13:1-22
18 -	Vengeance reaps its reward -- Violence	II Samuel 13:23-39
19 -	Reconciliation - sweet balm for a harried soul	II Samuel 14:1-33
20 -	The deception of disguised love	II Samuel 15:1-12; Psalm 62:1-12; Psalm 41:1-13
21 -	Split loyalties -- A blessing and a pain	II Samuel 15:13-28; Psalm 63:1-11
22 -	Bearing the grief to the mountain	Psalm 61:1-8; II Sam.15:29-37; Psalm 3:1-8
23 -	A prefigure of Calvary	Psalm 22:1-31
24 -	Only fools betray their friends	Psalm 14:1-7; 53:1-6 II Samuel 16:1-4

****

December 17 through December 24

Prepare yourself to follow the life of Solomon, David's son.
    How great the glory of Israel!   II Samuel 12:24-25.

Discuss the problem of love-sickness:
    Is love emotional? Over-emotional?
    Discuss love as a commitment: II Samuel 13.
    Discuss the problem of rape in today's society.

Discuss the problems of vengeance and violence, then and now.   II Sam. 13:23-39.
    Discuss Psalm 21 in the light of David and his son's experience.

Discuss the powers of reconciliation: II Samuel 14.
    Discuss the intrigue of deception: II Samuel 15.
    How do we see ourselves in this experience in our relationship to our
        heavenly Father?

How about the protection God gives in times of danger? Psalm 62:41.

A guide to praying for deliverance: Psalm 60:3.

Discuss Psalm 22 in its Messianic perspective.
    Is this a pre-figure of Calvary?
    In what way?

The betrayal of good friends is serious business with God: Discuss Psalms 14 and
    53 with that perspective in mind.

****

BIBLE READING GUIDE
    for BIBLE READING PEOPLE

December 25 - A leader of God's people   (Luke 2:11; Praise God!)
             in deep trouble   II Samuel 16:5-23; 17:1-24

        26 - Keep praying -- The Lord   Psalm 4:1-8; II Samuel 17:25-29;
             will hear   Psalm 42: 1-11

        27 - My heart hurts, Lord,   Psalm 43:1-5; 55:1-23
             Please listen

        28 - I'm counting on YOU, God,   Psalm 71:1-24
             Please don't let me down!

        29 - I'm slipping, Lord, save me,   Psalm 28:1-9; 143:1-12;
             Send your spirit speedily

        30 - God comes through!!   Psalm 40:1-17

        31 - A powerful message --   Psalm 701-5; 27:1-14
             for the close of the year

REFLECTIONS ON READINGS

December 25 through December 31

Take time off to meditate on the Christmas Story -- Luke 2:1-20.

Discuss the huge problems of being a leader in politics (government) in the light of II Samuel 16; 17; and 18.

Discuss the yearnings in the hearts of parents who share the difficulty of rebellious sons. Share thoughts from Psalms 4; 42; 43; and 55.

Discuss the problems of aging in the light of Psalms 71; 28:1-9; 143; and 40.

Share reflections on the close of another year: Psalm 70.

A solemn thought for the beginning of a new year: Psalm 27.

****

BIBLE READING GUIDE
for BIBLE READING PEOPLE   JANUARY (2nd Year)

January 1 - Floundering in deep trouble	Psalm 69
2 - Power - Peace, and a strange way to die	Psalm 121; II Samuel 18:1-18
3 - Mourning in mercy for a betrayer	II Samuel 18:19-33
4 - Grieve for a time, but get on with life	Psalm 10:1-18: II Samuel 19:1-10
5 - Peace and pardon among the hosts of God	Psalm 122:1-9; II Samuel 19:11-23; Psalm 92
6 - The King is come in peace - Blessing an old man	II Samuel 19:24-43
7 - Rebellion in the ranks again	II Samuel 20:1-22
8 - The voice of the Lord is more powerful than the vices of men	II Samuel 20:23-26; 21:1-14; Psalm 29:1-11

****

REFLECTIONS ON READINGS

January 1 through January 8

The main thrust, historically, is the struggle of David to maintain his kingdom in the face of the threat of his own son, Absalom. Vicious fighting ends with the tragic death of Absalom. (II Samuel 18:1-18)

In spite of Absalom's rebellion, David mourns grievously, even wishing that he
could have died in Absalom's place. (Compare Romans 9:3ff amd Exodus 32:32)
His bereavement carries him beyond reasonable mourning and General Joab
reprimands him for his unreasonable behavior. David responds and gets
back to the business of running the country. (II Samuel 19)

The Psalms read in relation to these traumatic events express mainly the deep
emotions of people in trouble. They express a manic-depressive swing of
the emotional pendulum. (e.g. Psalm 69). They lead to the high feelings
of God's presence and power (Psalm 121) and to the need and the joy to be
in God's presence in worship. (Psalm 122)

****

BIBLE READING GUIDE
for BIBLE READING PEOPLE

January 9 - The last war for the armies of David	Psalm 65:1-13; II Samuel 21:15-22; I Chronicles 20:4-8
10 - The last days of a great leader	Psalm 36:1-12; II Samuel 24:1-9; I Chronicles 21:1-6;
11 - Life is full of uneasy choices	I Chronicles 27:23-24; 21: 7-17; II Samuel 24:10-17
12 - An altar is raised to praise the Lord	II Samuel 24:18-25; I Chronicles 21:18-30; Psalm 30:1-12
13 - Sing to the end of your days	Psalms 33:1-22; 131:1-3; I Kings 1:1-9
14 - Conflicts for the king's throne	I Kings 1:10-37
15 - God is the King -- Sing his praises forever!	I Kings 1:38-53; Psalm 47:1-9;

****

REFLECTIONS ON READINGS

January 9 through January 15

The main theme continues with the decline of David's reign and the last wars
of his armies.

Some of the problems of frustration in this great leader are paricularly accented.

A contradiction -- Who led David to make the census? Satan? (I Chronicles 21:1)
or the Lord? (II Samuel 24:1)

How do you propose an explanation to the contradiction? Is God inconsistent? Would He ask people to do something and then punish them for doing it? (I Chron. 27:23-24; II Samuel 24:10-17). What are the answers to such difficult questions? Not even the commentaries come up with answers that satisfy human inquiry but do not probe the depths of the divine. Most important, even though we can't understand, confess the sin and seek God's mercy amd continue in worship. (II Samuel 24:18-25; I Chronicles 21:18-30)

In the midst of trouble, there is purpose for praise. When the epidemic was over they built an altar to the Lord. (II Samuel 24:18; I Chronicles 21:27ff.) They continued the Songs of Praise, (Psalm 33), and made confession of human inadequacies. (Psalm 131).

Psalm 33 amd I Kings 1:1-9 speak loudly to the fact that no one wins relying only on the strengths of powerful armies, war horses, or political intrigue. The result of such folly is division of families, friends, and even the fellowship of God's people in Christ.

****

BIBLE READING GUIDE
    for BIBLE READING PEOPLE

January 16 – The Lord's house must be exceedingly magnificent!	I Chronicles 22:1-19; 23:2-6
17 – The special office of the people's priests	I Chronicles 23:24-32; 24:1-31
18 – Music and song in the service of the Lord	I Chronicles 25:1-31
19 – Servants and officers of the "board"	I Chronicles 26:1-28
20 – Judges, Captains and Chiefs	I Chronicles 26:29-32; 27:1-22
21 – Get ready for a coronation	I Chronicles 27:25-34; 28:1-10; I Chronicles 23:1;
22 – Get ready for construction	I Chronicles 28:11-21; Psalm 145:1-21

****

REFLECTIONS ON READINGS

January 16 through January 22

I Kings 1:38-53: More struggles of kingship; people's involvement; family frustrations; loyalty and compassion in the heart of the king.

Psalm 47 is a reminder that whoever is the earthly ruler anointed for Kingship in Israel, the real KING is God himself. Psalm 97 parallels that thought. These are called ROYALTY PSALMS and were appointed to be read at the festive occasions of the coronation of kings. The remembrance of heritage is an important aspect in the Royalty Psalms. These psalms were also used on the Hebrew New Year's Day and referred to as "Yahweh's Enthronement". The rejection of the Lord as King bore with it serious consequences.... I Samuel 12;12 and following. Practical application for nations without the subjectivity of Kingship: -- Who calls the nations to account when the "state", whose royal kingship is "the will of the people", goes off on a tangent which reflects desertion of the Kingship of Jehovah?

> The tumult and the shouting dies;
>   The Captains and the Kings depart
> Still stands Thine ancient sacrifice,
>   An humble and a contrite heart.
> Lord God of hosts, be with us yet
> Lest we forget -- Lest we forget!

> Rudyard Kipling-Recessional - 1980

> Oh, Lord, it's hard to be humble
> When you're perfect in every way."

> Mac Davis -- 1979 (c)

The message changes significantly in the readings of Jan. 16-20. The key question is probably -- How important is worship and spiritual activity in the life of God's people? Note the material supply (I Chronicles 22) and the organizational structure of people and personnel. (I Chronicles 23 thru 28)

The departments included in their organization were:

Labor (workmen)   Temple officials (spiritual leaders)
Clerks (record keepers)   Music (vocal)
Judges (deciding disputes)   Security (temple guards)
Music (instrumental)   Treasury (gifts given to God)
Altar (sacred objects)   Agriculture (cattle and vineyards)
Maintenance (keeping things clean)   Education (King's family)
Bakery (wafers for offering)   Army Divisions

The week ends with a Psalm proclaiming the marvelous majesty and the unfailing faithfulness of the Almighty, Psalm 145, and with a solemn address of transition of responsibility from father to son. (David to Solomon, I Chronicles 28).

****

BIBLE READING GUIDE
    for BIBLE READING PEOPLE

January 23 - Bless the Lord with songs of   Psalm 104:1-35; 124:1-8
             praise

January 24 – The people gave, and that's praise, too!	Psalm 133:1-3; 86:1-17; I Chronicles 29:1-9
25 – The earnest prayer of a father for his son	I Chron. 29:10-19; Ps. 72:1-20
26 – Last words from father to son	I Chron. 29:20-22; II Sam. 23:1-7; I Kings 2:1-10
27 – Repast	I Chron. 29:28-30; Psalm 37
28 – All the kings shall praise THE KING	Psalm 138:1-8
29 – A good beginning for a new	I Kings 2:12-38; I Chronicles 29:23-25; II Chronicles 1:1

****

REFLECTIONS ON READINGS

January 23 through January 29

WORSHIP IS CENTRAL! Putting it into an illustration, church programming would look something like this:

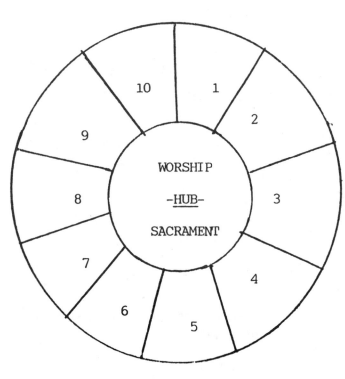

Anyone who has anything but a fleeting knowledge of the Word of God knows that the worship activity of God's people is the primary activity around which the spirit of church activity revolves. Anything other than that produces an imbalance which interferes with the smooth operation of people together in God's Kingdom program. Like the precisely balanced wheels on our cars, a bulge on the tire, a clod of mud, a bent rim, interferes in the operation and becomes an obstacle in the travel of the machine. The people in the car don't get to their destination without anxiety and delay. If the wheel is rightly balanced, it's a smooth trip all the way!

1 – Evangelism 6 – Choir
2 – Education 7 – Leaders
3 – Confirmation 8 – Retreats
4 – Visitation 9 – Trustees
5 – Social Service 10 – Council

Psalm 104:24 - All nature serves God - why shouldn't we?

Take note of the "Forensic Justification" (that is, declared innocent-- not proven innocent) in Psalm 24:5. Compare Romans 5:8-11; 5:16.

Psalm 133 - How sweet the harmony of fellowship:
        "There the Lord bestows His blessing" Vs. 3.

Look for Gospel accents in Psalm 86.
        e,g, vs. 5

Putting all that theology into practice
        The Giving - The Praising - The Thanking - I Chronicles 29

"We give Thee but Thine Own" - I Chron. 29:14. Lutheran Book of Worship #410.

Psalm 72 - Support your people of government with fervent prayer:
        (the end of David's prayers)

Vindication & Vengeance in David's dying days -- I Kings 2: 1-9.

Psalm 37 - Personal meditation & prayer for righteousness.

Psalm 138 - Thanksgiving for deliverance.

The NEW KING is on the throne -- Personal problems of paranoia & vengeance!
        I Kings 2:1-12ff. Contrast to I Chron. 29:25 and II Chron. 1:1.

****

BIBLE READING GUIDE
        for BIBLE READING PEOPLE

January 30 - A wise king goes to God for   I Kings 3:1-15; Ps. 45:1-17;
             wisdom   II Chronicles 1:2-13

        31 - Putting wisdom to work   I Kings 3:16-28; 11:21-22; 4:1-28

February 1 - The joyful anticipation of   I Kings 5:1-12; 7:13-14;
             building a temple for the Lord   II Chronicles 2:1-16

        2 - The workers - men and womem   I Kings 5:13-18; II Chron. 2:17-18
                                                  I Kings 2:39-46; Proverbs 31

        3 - Finishing of gold - the best   I Kings 6:1-22; II Chron. 3:1-9
            for God!

        4 - More gold and fine linen   I Kings 6:23-38; II Chron. 3:10-14;
                                                  Psalm 127; 128

        5 - The King's court and palace   I Kings 7;1-22; II Chron. 3:15-17

January 30 through February 5

How much trust can you put in dreams? Would Solomon have prayed otherwise if he were not dreaming? Dreaming or not, the prayer is a beautiful prayer. (I Kings 3:1-15) -- (II Chronicles 1:2-13). The gift of God's wisdom is immediate in the test of prostitutes. (I Kings 3:16ff & 4:29ff). Organization of personnel again is reflected in the early days of Solomon, leading to a prosperous reign. (I kings 4).

Alliances of nations is one of the most important issues of current politics. It was no different in the days of Solomon and historical alliances of the nation of Israel. "Solomon made an alliance with the King of Egypt.". How tremendous it would be today to hear the news, "There is peace in the Middle East!" -- a peace that could be trusted and even more effective than the Camp David alliances. (I Kings 3:1). An economic alliance with Tyre of Sidon, Through King Hiram is the announcement of I Kings 5:1; II Chronicles 2:11.

The insertion of Proverbs 31 in this context, in my estimation, is an error on the part of the chronological schedule that I have used to set up these readings. The lessons are interesting, nevertheless, and the first verse apropos for Solomon, too, since he ultimately ended up with a harem of 700 wives (Kings 11:3), who led to his eventual downfall.

Psalms 127 & 128 are the reminders of the reality that home (house) and family are truly blessed only when God is a part of it.

The personal reflections on Solomon's rule culminate in the unbelievable descriptions of the building of the grand and glorious temple, spanning a time of seven years and six months, built on Mt. Moriah. Note the first appearance of David, at Araunah's threshing floor, building an altar, to stop an epidemic. (II Samuel 24:18ff).

All the minute details of the building are covered in the parallel accounts of I Kings 5, 6, and 7 and II Chronicles 2 & 3 in this week's readings.

Can you imagine, in our day of automatic pressure tools which blast stone, rock and our ear drums, the fantastic accomplishment of constucting this glorious temple of the Lord without a single hammer blow? I Kings 6,7.

****

BIBLE READING GUIDE
    for BIBLE READING PEOPLE

February 6 - The intricacies of temple   II Chronicles 4:1-10;
         and palace   I Kings 7:23-37

      7 - Craftsmen and a lot of brass --   I Kings 7:38-51;
         and great beauty   II Chronicles 4:6-22

| February 8 - A glorious day of dedication | II Chronicles 5:1-14; I Kings 8:1-11 |

| 9 - Praise God and give thanks | Psalm 118:1-29; 115:1-18; 134:1-3; 136:1-26 |

| 10 - Solomon's sermon at the sanctuary | I Kings 8:12-21; II Chronicles 6:1-11 |

| 11 - Solomon's prayer in the presence of God and His people | I Kings 8:22-53 |

| 12 - A prayer for forgiveness and faithfulness | II Chronicles 6:12-42 |

****

REFLECTIONS ON READINGS

February 6 through February 12

The intricacies of the temple building and its furnishings are staggering to the imagination of thought and mind. It's obvious that the ornate style of the building with all its attending furniture and the Holy of Holies, containing the Ark of the Covenant, reflect the adoration that King Solomon and the people had for the glory of the Almighty.

To keep this in perspective, however, one must recall that this temple served the worshiping needs of several million people. The picture is completely different from today's circumstances. If, for example, all the people of a given metropolitan area were of one denomination, how grand and glorious a building they might build to the glory of God. Or, if all Lutherans were of one Synod, how great a temple headquarters might we build to serve the Church and through that, the Kingdom of God? (II Chronicles 6; I Kings 8)

Significantly, in the Psalms for this week's reading, we have basic theological accents relating to the New Testament and "Cornerstone Theology". For example, compare Psalm 118:22 with I Peter 2:7; and Psalm 118:20 with Revelation 21:25-27.

Theological questionmarks rise on the meanings and interpretations of texts such as Psalm 115:17. What was the understanding of "heaven" and "hell" in Old Testament theology? Compare Psalm 6:5; 30:9; 88:10-12 and Job 10:20-22.

Solomon's sermon and prayers are beautiful resources for meditation and devotion on the fellowship life of God's people, gathered for the purpose of growing in dedication and commitment to true worship and service of the Lord. (I Kings 8; II Chronicles 6; Colossians 1:8ff.)

LOOKING AHEAD:

The excitement and exaltation of worship in the temple brings exhilaration to the heart and soul. Get ready for an interesting picture language display of the romance of God with His people as shared in the love song of Solomon. It starts with the reading of February 16, -- a good postscript for Valentine"s Day

February 13 - The blessing and the benediction   I Kings 8:54-66; II Chron. 7:1-10;

          14 - Exaltation and Worship   Psalm 99:1-9;   I Kings 9:1-9;
               in the temple of the Lord   II Chronicles 7:11-12

          15 - Back to the business of   I Kings 9:10-14; II Chron. 8:1-3
               cities and kings

          16 - Of brides and bridegrooms   Song of Solomon 1,2,3, & 4

          17 - Love delayed and love fulfilled Song of Solomon 5 & 6

          18 - Love's triumph   Song of Solomon 7 & 8

          19 - The House of the Lord   I Kings 9:15-25; II Chron. 8:4-16
               is finished and USED!

****

REFLECTIONS ON READINGS

February 13 through February 19

The first portions of our reading bring to a close the high festival occasion of the dedication of the great temple at Jerusalem. (I Kings 8:54; II Chron. 7).

Interesting thoughts from Solomon's final prayer:
     "God kept His promises"
     "that we will always live as He wants us to live"
     "may He always be merciful" - "according to daily need"
     "may _you_ be faithful - obeying"

The immensity of sacrifice (Vs.62) - What a barbecue!

The Festival of Shelters - seven days - The Fall ingathering - (Review Exodus 23:17

How would you assess today's worship practices in the light of Exodus 23:17
     "Your _MEN_ must come to worship Me"

THE IMPORTANCE OF CHURCH ATTENDANCE BY FATHERS AND MOTHERS OF CHILDREN IN THE PARISH FAMILY TODAY -- (From a Time Magazine survey)

If both parents regularly attend church with their children, 77% of their children will remain faithful in church attendance as adults.

If only the father attends church with his children, 55% of those children will remain faithful. If only the mother attends church with her children, only 25% will remain faithful. If neither parent attends church with their children, only 6% will be faithful church attenders as adults.

****

It seems that parents and ESPECIALLY FATHERS are models in what they do whether they want to be or not. It also seems that the Biblical teachers knew what they were doing when they wrote of the fathers as having primary responsibility in the religious upbringing of their children.

Consider and discuss the interesting perspective on the JEWS as found in I Kings 9:9-19; also II Chronicles 7:11-22.

Interesting questions concerning the Jews to consider for discussion:

> Are the Jews, orthodox or otherwise, worshiping Jehovah today?

> Has God abandoned them through the course of history?
>> Give reasons for your answer.

> Do the passages cited above have the same credence as the promises of blessing?

> Which leads to the ultimate question: Why and how does God relate to the people of Israel and their problems today?

> Is there a difference between a "spiritual" Israel and a "geographic" Israel?

The Song of Solomon leads to deep questions of proper Scriptural exegesis or interpretation. Is it just poetry? Real - Romantic - Mystical - Lyrical??

Is it just a story, or does it have a message? Is it allegorical? Some suggested books for futher reference: "Learning to Use the Bible", and "Interpreting the Holy Scripture" - (Both published by Concordia Publishing House)

Allegory: A literary dramatic or pictorial representation; the apparent or superficial sense of which illustrates a deeper meaning.

Is it a parable?

Definition of parable: A natural story quite probable in experience but having a spiritual meaning.

Compare the New Testament parable of the "vineyard" (John 15).

"The theme of the book is love: pure, sensuous, youthful, passionate love. It is as old as the world and as new as today. It is echoed in literature and finds expression in Scripture. It begins in the Garden of Eden when man says, 'This is now bone of my bones and flesh of my flesh.' It appears in the teachings of Jesus. It is a mystery on the lips of Paul. (Ephesians 5:22ff.) It lingers on into the Revelation where the New Jerusalem comes down out of heaven 'prepared as a bride adorned for her husband'".
                              The Interpreter's Bible, Vol.V, Pg. 98

****

February 20 - National prosperity plus	I Kings 9:26-28; II Chron. 8:17-18; I Kings 10:1-13
21 - The splendor of Queens & Kings	II Chron.9:1-12; I Kings 10:14-25
22 - Prosperity and popularity hand-in-hand	II Chron.9:13-28; I Kings 10:26-29; I Kings 4:20-26; II Chron.1:14-17
23 - Wisdom, justice and mercy - ingredients for blessing	I Kings 4:29-34; Psalms 88 & 89
24 - The virtues of wisdom	Proverbs 1 & 2
25 - The wisdom of God and man	Proverbs 3 & 4
26 - The wisdom of good morals	Proverbs 5 & 6

****

REFLECTIONS ON READINGS

February 20 through Februaary 26

Never in the history of Israel have the people of God reached such a glorious pinnacle of triumph and prosperity. For 1000 years from the time of Abraham (Abram - Genesis 12) the chosen people of God, progenitors of the Christ, have experienced a gradual climb to glory. It's true--they had their ups and downs:

HIGH POINTS	LOW POINTS
Abram's call (Genesis 12)	400 years of slavery in Egypt
Joseph's rise to power (Genesis 41)	
The giving of the Law - Mt Sinai (Exodus 20)	The apostasy - (Exodus 32) The Golden Calf
The glory of the Tabernacle and the system of offerings. (Exodus & Leviticus)	The extended wandering from
The Priesthood & the Covenant Box (Ex.37)	Sinai to Palestine. (Numbers &
Entrance into the Promised Land (Joshua)	Deuteronomy
The Theocracy (Judges - Joshua)	Confusion in the land (Judges 21:25)
The rise of the kings:	The constant wars of Saul & David
Saul (40 years)	
David (40 years)	
Solomon (40 years)	Solomon turns from God (I Kings 11)
The permanent Temple in all its splendor and glory. (I Kings 8 - 10; II Chron. 7)	The tribes revolt (II Chron. 10)

Through it all: the guidance and judgment of God's LAW, with the presence of God's GOSPEL of mercy and grace, with constant forgiveness, are always evident.

The setting of Psalms 88 & 89 would be better in the context of King David's trials and tribulations, rather than in the time of Solomon. It is interesting to review Psalm 89 in the light of Messianic Prophecy. Compare the similarities of Psalm 89:26-52 and Hebrews Chapter I.

The Proverbs are so many and varied that it is practically impossible to provide a summarization and outline that does justice to the entire content of the book. A portion that deserves attention is God's rejection of those who refuse His counsel. E.g., Proverbs 1:22-32, specifically because it is so similar to the sin against the Holy Spirit. Compare Luke 12:8-10; Matthew 10:32-33 and 12:30-32 with the Proverbs text.

The wise sayings of Solomon are continued in our readings for another week. Look for those Proverbs which seem most appropriate to your personal needs.

****

BIBLE READING GUIDE
        for BIBLE READING PEOPLE

February 27	- Give wisdom the credit it deserves	Proverbs 7 & 8
28	- The benefits of wisdom and righteousness	Proverbs 9 & 10
29	- Putting knowledge into practice	Proverbs 11 & 12
March 1	- Wisdom is wealth; knowledge may be foolish	Proverbs 13 & 14
2	- The way of the wicked: vs. the way of the wise	Proverbs 15 & 16
3	- Good conduct is rewarding, and God-pleasing	Proverbs 17 & 18
4	- Better to be poor and right - than rich and wrong	Proverbs 19
5	- Justice and judgment are God's way to rightful honor	Proverbs 20 & 21

****

REFLECTIONS ON READINGS

February 27 through March 5

A penultimate question of Proverbs is, "Who is WISDOM?" - Answer:

        1 - WISDOM is a creation of God, therefore, not God Himself - Proverbs 8:22ff.
        2 - WISDOM is identified as a person -- Proverbs 9:1-3
        3 - WISDOM is identified as a female -- Proverbs 9:1-3

-62-

The first person referred to as "wise" (clever) was a woman, the woman of Tekoa (II Samuel 14:2).

The second person referred to as "wise" (clever) was a woman also, though unidentifed (II Samuel 20:16).

Solomon is given the gift of wisdom par excellence (I Kings 4:29-34).

In Jeremiah's time (Jeremiah 18:18) "wise men" giving counsel are listed in importance with the Prophets and Priests. Sometimes there are clashes. See Jeremiah 8:9 and Isaiah 29:14. Compare I Corinthians 1:18-25.

In general, "wisdom is synonymous with moral and religious intelligence; it is filled with strengthening ethical content." - Interpreter's Bible

****

BIBLE READING GUIDE
        for BIBLE READING PEOPLE

March 6 - The wise sayings of wise men   Proverbs 22 & 23

        7 - Watch out for the evil of envy   Proverbs 24

        8 - Wise steps to wise conduct   Proverbs 25

        9 - Sins of the slothful lead to   Proverbs 26 & 27
            sorrow and sadness

       10 - It is a good thing to have   Proverbs 28 & 29
            a righteous leader

       11 - The dilemma of being rich   Proverbs 30
            or poor

       12 - A great King slips from his   I Kings 11:1-14; 23-40
            glory

****

REFLECTIONS ON READINGS

March 6 through March 12

The PURPOSE OF PROVERBS is to recognize WISDOM - Proverbs 1:2.

        There is a distinct break in:

        1 - The wisdom literature: Chapters 1:7 through Chapter 9.
        2 - Solomon's Proverbs: Chapter 10 through Chapter 22:16.
        3 - The sayings of wise men:Chapter 22:17 through Chapter 24:34.
        4 - Solomon's Proverbs   Dhapter 25:1 through Chapter 29.

5 - Words of Agur (Chap. 30) and Lemuel (Chap. 30:1-9).
   Non-Israelite rulers of the Arabian Tribe of Massa - East of Palestine.
6 - The good wife - An acrostic; each verse begins with a successive
   letter of the Hebrew alphabet (Chap. 31:10-31).

Proverbs in the New Testament:

Proverbs 3:7	Romans 12:16b
Proverbs 3:11-12	Hebrews 12:5-6
Proverbs 3:34	James 4:6; I Peter 5:5b
Proverbs 4:26	Hebrews 12:13a
Proverbs 10:12b	I Peter 4:8b; James 5:20

Problems of Proverbs:

The inconsistencies of over-stated platitudes:

Proverbs 1:19; 3:2; 6:15; 10:3; 10:4; 11:31; 12:21;
        13:21; 14:14; 15:19; 22:4.

Compare with Jesus' statement in John 15:18-25; & 16:1-4.

The wisdom of Solomon (I Kings 4:29-34) is hard to understand in the light of
the foolish mistakes of his career and especially in his later life. (I Kings 11

****

BIBLE READING GUIDE
for BIBLE READING PEOPLE

March - 13 -	Life without purpose is peripheral piffle	Ecclesiastes 1:1-18; 2:1-11
14 -	Is life just vexation of spirit?	Ecclesiastes 2:12-26; 3:1-22;
15 -	Purpose for life comes with redemption through God' Son	Psalm 49
16 -	Oppression, poverty, and the inevitable end	Eccl. 4:1-16; 5:1-20; 6:1-12
17 -	Mankind's incurable evil nature	Ecclesiastes 7:1-29
18 -	God's providence is often a deep mystery	Ecclesiastes 8:1-17
19 -	Anarchy: the result of the the wrong set of values	Ecclesiastes 9:1-18; 10:1-20

****

March 13 through March 19

Ecclesiastes is a very puzzling book. It is a book with no Gospel, even though it is included in THE BOOK which is indeed, the Book of Hope for all mankind.

It might well be called "II Proverbs - The Negative Side."
Proverbs say, "Live right, love God, and you will prosper. Everything will turn out all right."

Ecclesiastes say, "Nothing works...try as hard as you can, but be prepared for the realities and disappointments, even disasters of life."

Some commentators go as far as to suggest that it is so foreign to Solomon"s thinking that there must have been another author who used the name of Solomon as a pseudonym. When the book was accepted into the Canon in 100 A.D., "it was preceded by a long controversy and the school of Hillel did not concur in the judgment of the school of Shammai, to whom the work was obnoxious....". Finally, it was admitted to Canonical rank because "Its beginning and its end are religious teachings." - Interpreter's Bible - Vol.V, Page 4

The Book of Ecclesiastes is a veritable obsession with pessimism:

          Chapter 1 - vs. 2,8.13,18
                  2 - Wisdom and accomplishment lead to nothing.
                      Vs. 11,14,20 -- Is life "just chasing the wind?"
                  3 - Everything is predestined -- Vs. 1-15.
                      The hoplessness of death and eternity - Vs. 16-21.
                  4 - Life is full of injustice - vs. 1 ff.
                      Better never to be born - Vs. 3. - Compare Job 3.
                  5 - Temple Worship respected - (A Positive) - Vs. 1-7.
                      Government oppression - Vs. 8-9.
                      Futility of high finance - Vs. 10-17.
                  6 - More injustice: Hopelessness in death.
                  7 - Proverbial sayings.
                  8 - A lesson for contemporary justice - Vs.11-14
                  9 - Same fate to the good and the bad; Another contemporary
                      lesson, vs. 18.
                 10 - More proverbial sayings - how true is vs. 5-6 today?
                 11 - The incomprehensible God! Vs. 5
                 12 - Advice to young -- assessment of "old", --
                      At least it's honest! Vs. 10.

Gleams of hope on the low horizon: 2:24; 4:9; 5:18; 8:15; 11:9; 12;1; 12:13.

In the midst of the gloom of Ecclesiastes, there is the Gospel of the Old Testament in Psalm 49:7-9. Compare Psalm 23 with Psalm 49:14.

Next week: Back to the reality of history.
            As history moves on for the nation of Israel, reflect on the history
            of our own country. What are the strong points of our historical
            development? What were and are some of our weaknesses?
            Dare we call them "sins"?

March 20 - The optimism of faith in God

Ecclesiastes 11:1-10; 12:1-14

    21 - The King is dead -- What now?

I Kings 11:41-43; II Chron.9:29-31
I Chronicles 3:10-24

    22 - The chronology of the 12 Tribes

Genesis 35:23-26;
I Chronicles 2:1-2; 4:1-23

    23 - Descendants and more descendants

Ruth 4:19-22
I Chronicles 2:9-55;

    24 - The descendants of Levi -
         The PRIESTS

Ezra 7:1-5
I Chronicles 6:1-30; 23:7-23

    25 - The Tribes of the songsters

I Chronicles 6:31-48;5:1-10;23-26;
Exodus 6:14

    26 - Issachar - Naphtali -
         Manasseh - Asher

Exodus 6:15
I Chronicles 4:24-38; 7:1-40

    27 - Benjamin - the youngest

I Chronicles 8:1-28; 9:1

****

REFLECTIONS ON READING

March 20 through March 27

The readings for this week reflect on the reign of Solomon (40 years) over the nation of Israel, his death, and the list of his descendants who succeeded him.

Review the "Chronology of the Bible" (e.g. Today's English Version, pages 373-375) Take note of where we have been and where we are going.

The readings review the 12 tribes, sons of Jacob, and the numbers and duties of the priests. The reading of Ezra 7 is significant in the fact that he was a descendant of Aaron, the High Priest.

Beginning with March 28, we read of the devastating national division which pursued Israel for the next 350-400 years.

With that reflection on history, our assignment, in addition to your reading, is to reflect on the history of our own country. What are the strong points of our historical development? What were ouor sins and weakness? QUO VADIS, AMERICA? Use a separate sheet to write down your personal views and assessments.

AMERICA'S

STRONG POINTS	WEAKNESS & WRONGS
THE POSITIVE SIDE	THE NEGATIVE SIDE

A CHRONOLOGICAL HISTORY
OF THE KINGS AND PROPHETS
OF THE DIVIDED KINGDOM

The Northern Kingdom ISRAEL	THE PROPHETS	The Southern Kingdom JUDAH
945 BC JEROBOAM (Solomon's Servant) 21 years Turns from God Established false priests and false worship	Time of constant war Unnamed Prophet of Judah I Kings 13 Old Prophet of Bethel,	REHOBOAM 945 (Solomon's Son) 17 years Arrogant, but faithful in worship
940 I Kings 13,33-34 Evil reign results in judgment from Shishak of Egypt	Prophet Ahijah I Kings 14 King Shishak (Egypt) Attacks and invades Judah	II Chronicles 10 940 Did what was evil No concern for the Lord's will II Chronicles 12,14 A time of sin and
935		prostitution 935 I Kings 14,22ff. Mixture of good and evil
930	400,000 Judah's Army defeats 800,000 Israelites Time of constant war I Kings 15,6	ABIJAH (ABIJAM 930 3years -- same sins as father I Kings 15 ASA Good king
925 NADAB (2years) Evil King		Peace for 10 years 925
BAASHA Rules 2 years EVIL LIFE	Time of Peace I Kings 14,1 10 years	Rules 41 years Plesed the Lord
920		Threw out the prostitutes 920 and pagan worship I Kings 15,9ff
915	Azariah's Prophecy II Chronicles 15	Invaded by Sudanese 915 Zerah, defeated by the Lord
910 905 Invades Judah	Drastic Prophet Jehu King Ben-Hadad I Kings 16	910 Defeats Israel II Chronicles 16
901 ELAH (1 year) Evil life	Prophet Hanani -- Seer II Chronicles 16,7	

901 BC ZIMRI (7 days)   901
       Evil - commits suicide
       OMRI (12 years)
       Sinned even more than
       those before him
895   Led people into sin   895
       I Kings 16,26
       GOD GETS ANGRY

890   AHAB (22 years)
       More and greater sins   ELIJAH
       Marries Jezebel   Conflict with Ahab
       Worships Baal   I Kings 17
       Bulds temple for   Flees for his life
       Baal worshipers   Fed Miraculouly
                               -- The Brook --
885   -- The widow --   JEHOSHAPHAT   885
                               Challenge to Baal   (25 years)
                               I Kings 18   Did what was right-
                               Beginning, and end   A good king
                               of drought   I Kings 22
                               BURN OUT - I Kings 19
                               OBADIAH (Not the prophet) Pagan worship
                                   Devout worshiper   allowed
                                   I Kings 18:3
                               Conflict with Ahab
                               Peace with Israel   Half-hearted worship 880
880   I Kings 22:44   II Chronicles 20:33
       Ahab's war   A brave king
       with Syria   I Kings 22:45
       I Kings 20
       The Lord wins! (vs,28)
875   The Naboth Story   875
       JUDAH   A time of peace with   ISRAEL
                               They join hands against Syria
                                   Pretending Prophets
                                   Deceptive MICAIAH
       Ahab's death   (I Kings 22)
       (I Kings 22:29ff)   Controversial Prophet Zedekiah
870   AHAZIAH (Son of Ahab)   (I Kinss 22)   870
       Evil - I Kings 22:51   Elijah prophesies - I Kings 22:24
       Ahaziah's death   II Kings 1:2; 9:27-28
       JORAM (II Kings 1:17) JEHU - Prophet to Judah
       (Brother to Ahaziah)   Rebukes the king
       Rules 12 years   II Chronicles 19:1-7
                               ELIJAH rebukes the king
865   II Chronicles 21:12ff   JEHORAM (8 years)   865

       Syria fights Israel   ELISHA succeeds ELIJAH   Married to Ahab's
       II kings 6   II Kings - the Bears   daughter
       Hazael succeeds   Edom revolts against   Evil king
       Benhadad (Syria)   Judah   Abandons God -
                                                         Leads people to sin
                                                         II Chronicles 21:10

                                  -68-

| 860 BC | | | Jehoram Joins Joram 860
War against Syria
II Chronicles 22:5 |

JEHU
Murders Joram
II Kings 9:23 ff.
Wipes out Baal
worship
855 Reigns 28 years.

Elisha anoints Jehu
II Kings 9:1 ff.

ATHALIAH (Queen)
Kills the royal family
Ruins the temple
A very corrupt woman
II Chronicles 24
855

JOASH
Saved from family murder
II Kings 11
7 years old
Pleased God
Reigns for 40 years
850 Faithful worshiper 850

850 **JEHOIADA**, the Priest
Restores faithful
Worship - II Kings 11:17

840 –20 years– 840

835 Temple rebuilt 835
II Chronicles 24:1-14

830 **JEHOAHAZ**
Rules 17 years
Leads Israel to sin
Trampled in dust
by Syrian enemies

830
After Jehoiada dies
Joash reverts to
idol worship
II Chronicles 24:17ff.

825 Israel oppressed by
Syrian kings Hazael
and Benhadad
II Kings 13:22 ff.

825
Joash assassinates
the prophet Zechariah
II Chronicles 24:21ff.

815 **JEHOASH**
Rules for 16 years
Sins against the Lord
Like Jeroboam (1st King)
Bravery in war

815
Syria attacks Judah
II Kings 24:23ff.
Joash dies an
assassin's death

WAR BETWEEN ISRAEL AND JUDAH

AMAZIAH
II Kings 14:1ff.
Rules 29 years

810 Visits Elisha

Elisha dies
II Kings 13:14
Called "Mighty Defender"
by Jehoash

Pleased the Lord 810
but allowed pagan
worship
Fights and defeats
Edom - challenges

805
Israel to fight 805
but is defeated

800 BC Jehoash captures Amaziah in battle II Chronicles 25:23 & II Kings 14:3 ff		Jerusalem looted by Israelite King Jehoash 800

800 BC Jehoash captures
Amaziah in battle
II Chronicles 25:23 &
II Kings 14:3 ff

Jerusalem looted
by Israelite King
Jehoash   800

Amaziah captured
by Jehoash
II Chronicles 25:23

795 JEROBOAM II
Rules fo 41 years
Sins against God
II Kings 14:23 ff.

The Prophet AMOS

UZZIAH (Or Azariah)   795
Son of Amaziah
Rules 52 years
Pleases the Lord, BUT
permits pagan worship

Contradicts the
Priest, Amaziah
Amos 7:10

Serious skin disease
Son, Jotham, governs
Zechariah,   790
religious adviser
to the King.
II Chronicles 26:5
Fights the   785
Philistines with
God's help
II Chronicles 26:7-8

790   Amos, Prophet to Israel

785

775   HOSEA, the Prophet   775

770   ISAIAH   770
Prophecies through the
history of four kings
Isaiah 1:1

765 ZACHARIAH   765
Reigns only 6 months
SHALLUM (only 1 month)
760 MENAHEM   760
Assassinates Shallum
A vicious defeat
Rules 10 years
     Invasion of
     Tiglath-Pileser III
     of Assyria
755 Dies in gross sinfulness   755
Bribes Tiglath-Pileser
with money from the rich

750 PEKAHIAH - 2 year reign   750
Assassinated

ASSYRIA THE WORLD POWER

PEKAH
Rules 20 years

JOTHAM
Reigns 16 years
A GOOD KING

745   745

TIGLATH-PILESER TAKES THE FIRST WAVE OF ISRAELITES CAPTIVE

745 BC	MICAH, the Prophet Contemporary of Isaiah Prophet to Judah Message: Judgment - Mercy - HOPE	745
735	ISAIAH THE PROPHET Record Keeper II Chronicles 26:22 Prophecies through the time of Hezekiah	735
730	The Prophet OBED II Chronicles 28:9	AHAZ 730 20 years old Rules 16 years An evil King Sacrifices his son to pagan worship

HOSHEA

725	Assassinates Rekah Shalmanezer of Assyria attacks Israel Israel becomes subject to Assyrian power Rebels -- but is conquered! Hoshea is imprisoned	HEZEKIAH 725 Pleased the Lord Destroys pagan altars Rebels against Assyrian aggression and is successful They reopen the Temple
720	THE FALL OF ISRAEL	720
700		MANNASSEH 700 12 years old Rules 55 years Lived a disgusting way of life.
645		AMON 645 22 years old Reigned 2 years Gross sinner Assassinated
640	Zephaniah predicts doom and destruction also upon Judah	JOSIAH 640 8 years old Ruled 31 years

635 BC	NAHUM-The Prophet	(Josiah continued) 635
	Prophecies concerning the destruction of Ninevah	Worshiped God Smashed the altars (Also called Jehoahaz) 23 years old Only a 3 months reign
620	JEREMIAH The great Prophet	620
615	ZEPHANIAH Contemporary of Jeremiah	615
610		610

BABYLON -- THE WORLD POWER

605		JEHOIAKIM 605 25 years old 11 year reign sinned greatly
600		JEHOIACHIN 600 18 years old Reigns 3 months 10 days
595		(MATTANIAH) 595 Changed to ZEDEKIAH Reigns 11 years
	Hanniah A Minor Prophet	Wouldn't listen to the Lord
585	OBADIAH The last voice of warning	585
		THE FALL OF JERUSALEM!

The readings that follow represent the separate histories of the divided kingdom.

Revolution and divisions split the national unity.

ISRAEL'S TEN TRIBES (The Northern Kingdom)	JUDAH'S TWO TRIBES (The Southern Kingdom)
March 28 II Chronicles 10:1-19; I Kings 12:1-20 Jeroboam becomes king	March 28 Rebellion Rehoboam rules
March 29	March 29 I Kings 14:21; II Chron.12:13-16 Idolatry rules
March 30 The ALTAR ABUSED	March 30 I Kings 12:21-24; II Chron.11:1-23 Apostasy is rampant
March 31	March 31 II Chron.12:1-12; I Kings 14:19-24 The Prophet speaks Repentance returns
April 1 I Kings 13:33-34 Persistence in evil	April 1 I Kings 13:1-32 Wickedness abounds
April 2 I Kings 14:1-18 Dealings of Darkness and Death	April 2 I Kings 14:25-28 Invasions from Egypt

****

REFLECTIONS ON READINGS

March 28 through April 2

Consider and discuss:
Is force always the better solution? Was it God's fault? Youth vs. sage advice of
the elder. Are events of history predestined to happen because God has already
plannned them? These are questions that rise from the reading of II Chronicles 10:1-1

What credence would you put on I Kings 12:19 as relevant for today?

The gullibility of people engaged in false worship - I Kings 12:25-33

The impertinence of worship: Site contemporary situations of which you may be aware

A prophet's perplexing power- and predicament: I Kings 13: II Chronicles 16:10

The importance of confessing sin: The problem of pretension in the presence of God
        I Kings 14:7ff.

BIBLE READING GUIDE
    for BIBLE READING PEOPLE

Israel's Ten Tribes-Northern Kingdom | Judah's Two Tribe-Southern Kingdom

April 3
I Kings 14:30
Civil War (North vs. South)

April 3
I Kings 15:1-2 & 6; 14:29-31
II Chronicles 12:13-16; 13:1-2
Constant Warfare - Change of kings

April 4
II Chronicles 13:3-19
Thousands against Thousands

April 4
II Chron. 13:20-22; I Kings 15:3-8
Sins from generation to generation

April 5
I Kings 14:19-20; 15:25-28
Unrighteous rulers

April 5
II Chron. 14:1-8; I Kings 15:9-11
Reformation and peace

April 6
I Kings 15:29-34
The evil life of sinful kings

April 6
II Chron.14:9-15;15:1-7; Psalm 77
God blesses with victory

April 7
(no reading)

April 7
II Chron.15:8-19; I Kings 15:12-15
Reforms in worship
Rejuvenation in spirit

April 8 - 901 B.C.
I Kings 15:16;   II Chronicles 16:1-6
Leagues and Alliances

April 8
I Kings 15:17-22 & 32
The wars resume

April 9
I Kings 16:1-20
The Prophet against the Prince

April 9
II Chronicles 16:7-10
Warnings from the prophets

****

REFLECTIONS ON READING

April 3 through April 9

II Chronicles 13 - The largest army doesn't always win - II Chronicles 14:10 ff.

How earnestly do we try to find the Lord's will in our lives? Personally?
    Congregationally? Denominationally? Nationally? Review II Chronicles 16:9

Do we become "stale" in worship? What changes would you recommend? II Chron.15:8-19

Important things to pursue in the coming readings are not just the chronological data,
but to search for spirituality or lack of it, in the minds of rulers and the the
people themselves. Look for those moods and conditions in the minds of the people.

Then study the characteristics of our own spirituality? What is spirituality, really?

BIBLE READING GUIDE
      for BIBLE READING PEOPLE

April 10 (Israel)   April 10 (Judah)
I Kings 16:21-29 - 900 B.C.   (no reading)
Division within the divisions

April 11   April 11
I Kings 16:30-34; 21:25   I Kings 15:23-24; 22:41-46
Idolatrous living leads to   II Chronicles 16:11-14; 20:31-34
idolatrous worship   Disease and death

April 12   April 12
I Kings 17:1-16; 18:4   II Chronicles 17:1-19; 18:1
Prophecy is not without risk   The right way of a righteous ruler

April 13   April 13
I Kings 17:17-21; 18:1-15   (no reading)
The miracle of resurrection (O.T.)

April 14   April 14
I Kings 18:16-39 - 879 B.C.   (no reading)
The contest at Carmel

April 15   April 15
I Kings 18:40-46; 19:1-9   (no reading)
The rain settled it

April 16   April 16
I Kings 19:10-18   (no reading)
A big God speaks in a small voice

****

REFLECTIONS ON READINGS

April 10 through April 16

As we assess politics in today's world it is my contention that "the good old days"
of the Old Testament reveal that ours are the better days. What do you think?

Discuss the problems of Civil War -- Israel's compared to the Civil War of the USA?

Assess the times Ahab (I Kings 16:29ff) and Omri (I Kings 17:21ff) How evil were they?

Asa rules for 41 years in Judah and the land is blessed with 10 years of peace. He
defeats Israel and also drives out Benhadad, a Syrian monarch.   I Chronicles 16.

Interwoven with the struggles of the kings are the subtle (sometime not so subtle)
messages and influence of the prophets Jehu (north) and Hanani (south).
Review I Kings 16 and II Chronicles 16:17.

What religious leaders do you think are the greatest influence on American society?
On the world scene?

Discuss the price that prophets sometimes pay for their activity:
II Chronicles 16:10; I Kings 18:4; 19:1 ff.
Discuss the possibility of religious leaders being at risk today?

Review the relationship of Elijah and Ahab -- I Kings 17
The prophet sustained by a miracle
Impact of the story of the widow of Zarephath - I Kings 17 vs.8ff
Consider Elijah's prayerful struggle with God

Consider the proof of God's promise in resurrection -
Compare I Kings 17:23-24 with Hebrews 1:1-3

CONSIDER AND DISCUSS - If the kind widow of Zarephath was convinced of Elijah's credibility because of the resurrection of her son, HOW MUCH MORE OUGHT WE BE CONVINCED OF THE CREDIBILITY OF GOD'S MESSAGE BECAUSE OF THE RESURRECTION OF HIS SON!

The intrigue of the great BAAL debate -- Review I Kings 18
An important question for any generation - vs.21
The call for PROOF from God -vs. 36: How do people repeat that today?
The first known clergy burn out -- I Kings 19:4
Interesting questions for our perusal -
What are the modern Baals of our present world?
"what are YOU doing here? - I KIngs 19:9-13

****

BIBLE READING GUIDE
for BIBLE READING PEOPLE

April 17 (Israel)
I Kings 19:19-21
One prophet to another

April 18
I Kings 20:1-21
A new set of wars

April 19
I Kings 20:22-34
Count two for Israel

April 20
I Kings 20:35-43; 22:1
Ashes to Ashes - Life for Life

April 21
I Kings 21:1-29
Death and doomsday for Israel

April 22
I Kings 22:2-4 - 870 B.C.
Re-alliance between North and South

April 17 (Judah)
(no reading)

April 18
(no reading)

April 19
(no reading)

April 20
(no reading)

April 21
(no reading)

April 22
II Chronicles 18:2-3
Reunion of old tribes

April 23
I Kings 22:5-12

April 23
II Chronicles 18:4-5; 9-11

THE PROPHETS PRETEND

****

REFLECTIONS ON READINGS

April 17 through April 23

The week's readings continue to present the interaction of the prophets and the kings. In today's terminology we would see it as the cross-over influence between the Church and the State. Discuss this principle and how it is applied today?

Elisha is called as successor to Elijah. Compare the two. I Kings 19:19-21

A prophet becomes the "Secretary of War" with Ahab"s struggle against Syria"s Benhadad. (I Kings 20:16). Is this where General George Washington got hlis inspiration for crossing the Delaware on Christmas Eve? Discuss the possibilities of religious men and women serving in political leadership positions.

The bold stance of a little man (Naboth). I Kings 21.
    Discuss the current application -- "You can't fight city hall!"
    Ahab's repentance wins a reprieve. (Vs.27ff.)

A good decision: Both kings, Ahab (Israel) and Jehoshaphat (Judah) decide to
    consult the Lord. I Kings 22:5

****

BIBLE READING GUIDE
for BIBLE READING PEOPLE

April 24 (Israel)
I Kings 22:13-28

April 24 (Judah)
II Ch;ronicles 18:6-8; 12-27
Finding the RIGHT prophet isn't easy

April 25
I Kings 22:29-40

April 25
II Chronicles 18:28-34
A King's deception leads to his death

April 26
(no reading)

April 26
II Chronicles 19:1-7; Psalm 82

April 27
(no reading)

April 27
II Chronicles 19:8-11
Restoration of relationship with God
through restoration of justice

April 28
(no reading)

April 28
II Chronicles 20:1-13
The King turns to prayer

April 29	April 29
(no reading)	Psalm 83
	A prayer fit for a king

April 30	April 30
(no reading)	II Chronicles 20:14-19

****

REFLECTIONS ON READINGS

April 24 through April 30

More influential activity by the prophets - I Kings 22
>   Discuss the hostility toward Micaiah - (vs. 8)
>   Is it different today? Express your reasons for your answer.
>   "You shouldn't say that!" - Don't you just hate people using that expression?

Read Well!
>   Look for the overtones of the Book of Revelation - I Kings 22:19
>   Prophecy fulfilled: Ahab's end as predicted - I Kings 21:17-19
>   Study the parallel - II Chronicles 18

For several days our emphases has been on Israel — Ahab - Northern Kingdom
Emphases will now shift to Judah -- Southern Kingdom - II Chronicles 19

An honest assessment by a prophet, Jehu - II Chronicles 19:1-7
>   Jehoshaphat responds with reforms - II Chronicles 19:4
>   How did this effect the Judges (civil leaders) and the Levites - (priests)?
>   Warning appropriate to contemporary society:
>   Consider the divisions between religious and civil cases.

Psalm 82 - Consider how God and "justice in the land" relate to one another

Living under the threat of invasion
>   The King leads in prayer - II Chronicles 20

The awesome content of the imprecatory prayers - e.g. Psalm 83
>   Under what circumstances could we ever pray with this spirit — if ever?
>   A thought to consider: Praying this prayer is impossible except in the
>   context of direct opposition of good (Kingdom of God) and evil. (Satan inspired)

****

BIBLE READING GUIDE
>   for BIBLE READING PEOPLE

May 1	May 1
(no reading)	Psalm 46
	Don't be afraid-God is our Refuge

May 2	May 2
(no reading)	II Chronicles 20:20-26
	Praise the Lord, pass the ammunition

May 3
(no reading)

May 3
II Chronicles 20:27-28; Psalm 48
Rejoice in the victory

May 4 - (870 B.C,)
I Kings 22:51-53; II Kings 1:1-2; 3:4-5
Another evil king

May 4
II Chronicles 20:29-30
Peace and quiet in the kingdom

BRIEF ALLIANCE BETWEEN THE KINGDOMS

May 5
II Chronicles 20:35-37; II Kings 1:3-18
A man of God confronts a man of the people

May 5
I Kings 22:44-49
Jehoshaphat makes peace -- and dies

May 6 -- 869 B.C.
II Kings 3:1-3
Improved -- but still evil

May 6
(no reading)

May 7
II Kings 2:1-11
A dramatic parting

May 7
(no reading)

****

REFLECTIONS ON READINGS

May 1 through May 7

Psalm 46 - The scource and inspiration for Luther's Reformation Hymn. "A MIGHTY
FORTRESS IS OUR GOD". Study the hymn -- sing it together in your class.
     Was this a glimpse of Revelation 21:10ff? Check it out.

Back to music and marching to the Lord's tune -- II Chronicles 20:20-30
     Better believe those prophets!

Ahaziah succeeds Ahab (Northern Kingdom) -- just as bad - rules only 2 years
     Brief alliance ends in catastrophe -- II Chronicles 20:35ff; I Kings 22:48-51

The prophets's message supported with traumatic events -- II Kings 1:3ff

Joram succeeds Ahaziah -- a better king --II Kings 3:1-3

The first ASCENSION -- Elijah -- II Kings 2:1
     The power transmitted --
     Compare this with the ASCENSION of Christ - Acts. 1

Did you know that the total destructive power of all bombs of World War II plus the
Veitnam war was 7,000 Kilotons?

Did you know that the total U.S. and Soviet long range nuclear arsenal is equal to
11,089,000 Kilotons? or - 1,584 times the power of the explosives used in all of
World War II and the Vietnam War combined? (1984 statistic)

A MODERN DAY PSALM 46

1.- God is our shelter and strength
      Always ready to help in time of trouble.

2 - So we will not be afraid, even if the earth is threatened
      and shaking from the threats of nuclear warheads.
      Mountains will become seas from the power of the explosions.

3 - Seas will foam from the violence of nuclear waste.

4 - Yet there will be a pure stream of God's mercy that will
      bring nourishment and strength to those who live in the
      permanent City of God.

5 - That city will be secure from all nuclear bombing.
      It will never be destroyed.
      God will bless every morning with peace.

6 - Nations will be terribly frightened.
      Old kingdoms will shake.
      God thunders ... the earth will be no more.

7 - But the Lord Almighty is with us.
      The God of old Jacob is our refuge.

8 - Come and see what the Lord has done:
      It is amazing what He has done to the earth!

9 - Wars are all over now.
      Bows and spears and rifles and fighting planes and the powerful missiles
      with nuclear detonation are all burned out -- except in Hell.

10- No more need to fight.
      I AM IN CONTROL. Just know that I AM GOD -
          I AM that I AM, THAT's ALL!

11- The Lord Almighty is with us.
      The God of old Jacob is still around.
      He is and always will be
      My shelter from the ravaging radiation which has destroyed the earth.
      He is the forever Refuge.

                                        Leo E. Wehrspann (1983)

****

BIBLE READING GUIDE
     for BIBLE READING PEOPLE

May 8 (Israel)   May 8 (Judah)
II Kings 2:12-25   (no reading)
The ministry of a new prophet

                FORCES OF THE TWO KINGDOMS JOINED

<u>May 9</u> (Israel) 868 B.C.	<u>May 9</u> (Judah) II Kings 3:6-20 Music inspires a message
<u>May 10</u> (no reading)	<u>May 10</u> II Kings 3:21-27; 4:1-7

<u>TOGETHER, THERE IS A CONQUERING</u>

<u>May 11</u> II Kings 4:8-17 A son is born by prophesy	<u>May 11</u> II Kings 8:16-17; 22:45 & 50 II Chronicles 20:34; 21:5 Death brings drastic change
<u>May 12</u> II Kings 4:18-37 The miracle of resurrection The son restored by the prophet	<u>May 12</u> II Chronicles 21:1-4; 6-7; & vs.11; II Kings 8:18-19 God keeps His promises -- in spite of the evil of man
<u>May 13</u> (no reading)	<u>May 13</u> 864 B.C. Obadiah 1:1-9 The eagle flies high -- BUT
<u>May 14</u> II Kings 8:1-2; 4:38-44 Famine and "Death in the Pot" -	<u>May 14</u> Obadiah 1:10-20 Sins of nations are not overlooked

****

<u>REFLECTIONS ON READINGS</u>

May 8 through May 14

The new Prophet and his ministry -- II Kings 2:14 ff.

    <u>MIRACLES</u>

        What is the message? II Kings 2:19-22
        Cleansing water -- Baptism?
        Cleansing blood -- The Cross?
            The Message is -- <u>POWER TO CLEANSE</u>
            Be sure to read <u>I John 1:8-10</u>

The Prophet curses? II Kings 2:23-25
        Compare: II Chronicles 16:22 and Psalm 105:1-5

More miracles -- II Kings 2:38ff. -- Compare Luke 9:10ff.

Wars and prophets -- II Kings 3

Concern for a widow in poverty -- II Kings 4:1-7
        By contrast -- A rich woman desires a blessing -- II Kings 4
        Life, death, and resurrection -- Consider New Testament -- Luke 7:11ff.
        Jesus exercises His power over death -- raises the widow's son

(Reflections continued)

The end of Jehoshaphat's reign - I Kings 22:45-50; II Chronicles 20:34

The strength of God's promise - II Kings 8:16-19; II Chronicles 21:5-7

****

THE PARALLELS OF TIME

THE PAST	THE PRESENT	THE FUTURE TIMES
OLD ISRAEL	THE NEW ISRAEL	THE NEW ISRAEL
The Kingdom of Israel	(Beginnings)	The Kingdom of Israel
Geographically - O.T.	The Church between	The Church Triumphant
The Church in preparation	great times	IN GLORY - HEAVEN
PRE-CHRIST	CHRIST-PRESENT	CHRIST-PRESENT
	(Visible/Invisible)	(Visible)

****

BIBLE READING GUIDE
   for BIBLE READING PEOPLE

May 15 (Israel)
II Kings 5:1-27
A Captain - sick and saved

May 16
(no reading)

May 17
II Kings 6:1-23
Iron floats?

May 18
II Kings 6:24-33
Gruesome murderers

May 19
(no reading)

May 20
II Kings 7:1-20
Now hear the Word of the Lord

May 21
II Kings 8:3-15
After the famine -- RESTORATION

May 15 (Judah)
II Kings 8:20-22; II Chron. 21:8-10
Revolt and insurrection

May 16
II Chronicles 21:12-17; Sickness
signaled thru mysterious predictions

May 17
(no reading)

May 18
II Chronicles 21:18-20
II Kings 8:23-25; 9:29
Dreadful sickness

May 19
II Kings 8:26-27
One year op evil

May 20
II Chronicles 22:1-4
A Mother's bad counsel

May 21
(no reading)

REFLECTIONS ON READINGS

May 15 through May 21

This week's readings have a wide gamut of thought for reflections:

1 - The interesting story of Naaman shows the intense way in which God sometimes uses different modes, moods, and people to get to the solution of
   problems in the minds and hearts and lives of people. (II Kings 5)

    Note: The people involved - Naaman, the <u>victim,</u> a great soldier
                             Naaman's wife
                             A little Israelite girl, a <u>captive</u>
                             The Prophet Elisha
                             The King of Syria
                             The King of Israel
                             Servants

<u>Modes and Means</u>
Conversations, letter writing, gifts and offerings, horses and chariots,
and the water of the Jordan.

<u>Moods</u>
King of Israel-"Am I God?"-"I can't do that!"-dismay and despair, suspicious
The Prophet Elisha - confidant
Naaman -- rage, looks for the spectacular, insulted, felt rejected and
               humiliated -- converted
The servants - remonstrative

<u>All this to heal one man!</u>

SUMMARIZATION: <u>God can heal instantly, BUT</u> - Most often, God will use people
means and material, and whatever He may choose to accomplish His purpose

2 - <u>The Sequel:</u> The danger of trying to capitalize on God's production
   A mixture of wars and their consequences - II Kings 8:20-22
   Killed with kindness - II King 6:8-23; II Chronicles 21:8-10
   The enemy is spared - (A reversal from previous onslaughts, II Kings 6:24-
   7:20).   THE LORD DID IT AGAIN!
   The "meddling" prophet again -- Elijah - II Chronicles 21:12-17
   Mind over matter and ESP -- II Kings 6:1-6; 5:26
   <u>Don't Hide the good news</u> -- II Kings 7:8-9 -- Don't gobble up grace
   without sharing the bounty of the Gospel.

****

<u>BIBLE READING GUIDE</u>
    <u>for BIBLE READING PEOPLE</u>

<u>In Unity There Is Power and Healing</u>

<u>May 22</u>
II Kings 8:28-29; 9:1-13
The anointing of another king

<u>May 22</u>
II Chronicles 22:5-6
Judah joins Israel in war

May 23 (Israel)   May 23 (Judah)
II Kings 9:14-26   II Chronicles 22:7
          Conspiracy, Treachery and Tyranny among the Kings

May 24   May 24
II Kings 9:27-29   II Kings 11:1-3; II Chron. 22:8-10
          Royalty no guarantee against chicanery

May 25 - 857 B.C.   May 25
II Kings 9:30-37; 10:1-11   II Chronicles 22:11-12 - Saved from
Jezebel's violent reward   the slaying by a sister's sympathy

May 26   May 26
II Kings 10:12-28 (Vs.15)   II Kings 11:4-12
Heart to heart -- Hand to hand   Attention to the Lord's House
                                         brings peace to the land

May 27   May 27
II Kings 10:29-33   II Chronicles 23:1-11
Backsliding again   Gathering the congregation

May 28   May 28
(no reading)   II Kings 11:13-16
                                         The wickedness of the King's mother
                                         repaid with a wicked end

****

REFLECTIONS ON READINGS

May 22 through May 28

NO ELECTION --   The PROPHET APPOINTS AND ANOINTS
        The King - Jehu replaces Ahaziah in the Northern Kingdom (Israel) II Kings 9

        The Lord did the choosing - II Chronicles 22:7ff

        The Prophet - ONE OF THE CRAZIES?? II Kings 9:11

Forerunner of Palm Sunday - II Kings 9:13; Compare Matthew 21
        Christ, the combination of PROHET AND KING - Matthew 21:5 and 11
                Also PRIEST - Hebrews 4:14; 5:10

A religious war -- II Kings 9:14ff; 10:12ff: II Chronicles 22:7ff
        Gruesome massacres -- II Kings 10:6ff
        "The Hiding Place" - saved by a sister - II Kings 11:2-3; II Chron. 22:11-12

Consider the importance of Temple Worship -- II Kings 11:4ff
        It brings peace
        Worship even with the protection of armed guards

        But always the backsliding -- II Kings 10:29-33
                Why worship with half a heart?
                Why does it happen -- Discuss today's circumstances
                The analyses of Jesus, our Lord - Luke 8:11-15

-84-

THE NORTHERN KINGDOM ISRAEL	THE SOUTHERN KINGDOM JUDAH
May 29 (no reading)	May 29 II Chronicles 23:12-21; 24:1-3 II Kings 11:17-20; 12:1-3 Righteousness leads to revival
May 30 II Kings 10:34-36; 13:1-7 & 22 The end of another reign	May 30 II Chronicles 24:4-7; II Kings 12:4-8 Faithless priests fail in their duty
May 31 (no reading)	May 31 II Kings 12:9-16: II Chron.24:8-14 The TEMPLE is restored as the TREASURY is filled
June 1 (no reading)	June 1 Joel 1 -- Natural catastrophies re- flect God's judgment. (Special note- It is uncertain whether Joel was a pre-exilic or a post-exilic prophet. While the time of his ministry may not be important, his MESSAGE is!
June 2 (no reading)	June 2 Joel 2 -- Repent in preparation for the Lord's return
June 3	June 3 Joel 3 -- The Lord's victory is the undoing of the enemy
June 4 II Kings 13:8-11 A good reign undone by an evil king..	June 4 - 820 B.C. II Chronicles 24:15-22 -- The death of a good man - followed by evil

****

REFLECTIONS ON READINGS

May 29 through June 4

The young king, Joash, 7 years old -- saved by a sister
       A contemporary parallel -- Corrie Ten Boom -"The Hiding Place"
       Rules for 40 years in Judah -- Pleases the Lord
       Repairs the temple -- How well do we maintain our worship building?
       Collects money -- So what's new with a building fund?
       Review the Temple dedication and the joy that went with it - I Kings 8:10
       The temple is now 143 years old - 972 to 829 B.C.
       Recall and share your most memorable "church building/dedication experience?

Jehoiada - <u>Priest</u> in charge -- II Chronicles 24:6
    Good leader - faithful priest - 130 years old -
    After his death people fell away. II Chronicles 24:14-18

Jehu -- (Isarael) dies after 28 year reign -- II kings 10:34-36

Jehoahaz becomes king and stirs up God's anger against Israel - II Kings 13:1-7

Strange circumstances in Elisha's death -- II Kings 13:-14-20

****

A <u>new prophet</u> on the scene -- <u>JOEL</u>   (828 B.C.

Consider the following assessment of Joel --
    <u>Interpreter's Bible</u>, Vol.VI, Pages 736-737

"Joel 1:1-3: The Present Distress, except in unusually tranquil and optimistic times
every generation tends to think that its trouble exceeds anything humanity has known
before. It is easy to capitalize on this fact in order to descredit the so-called
"prophets of gloom" and discount their warnings. How often ruin has been predicted
and yet mankind still survived! How often the end of the world has been foretold,
and yet the world is still here!

Joel, however, does not shrink from painting the calamity of his day in the darkest
colors possible. He begins by implying that the present visitation of locusts has
no precedent,and is unlikely to be paralleled in the future. The devastation is such
that it cannot be surpassed. This is more than rhetorical flourish meant to command
attention; and it is not to be understood as the extravagance of a habitual
pessimist. For the point is not really whether the plague in Joel"s time was the
worst that his country ever suffered. Suffering cannot be measured by   statistics.
Calamities cannot be compared in any but the most superficial manner. The trouble
of the moment is the one that men have to reckon with, and it cannot be brushed
aside by reference to troubles of other days. Where ever suffering and evil exist,
there is a situation which demands to be faced in its full gravity.

The Scriptures recognize with complete seriousness the reality of evil. The gulf
between despair and faith is not crossed by ignoring the somber facts of human
life. It is crossed only when the troubles of humanity are first seen as the
consequence of man's fall ...... The sufferings of the world must be recognized as
acts of divine judgment. For then the avenue of repentance may be opened up,
whereby healing is to be found. Our cure must come from the hand that has smitten
us. Such is the theme of Joel."

Again, we face the uncertainty of the time of Joel's presence. The "Chronological
Bible", from which we get our reading sequence, places it before the exile. Most
commentators and other scholars suggest a much later date, even after the Exile. The
prophetic message, however, is most appropriate in either setting. His love of
worship and respect for the Temple gained for him the description, "<u>TEMPLE - PROPHET</u>
rather than priest.

As you read, look for the <u>LAW</u> - <u>GOSPEL</u> themes and share them in discussion.

Questions for further consideration:

    1 - Could Amos' description of locusts from the north destroying the land be a
        figurative description of the hordes of Babylonian armies? Amos 2:20-25
    2 - Obviously, Joel's prediction is fulfilled in the New Testament with the
        Pentecost scene. Discuss Acts 2:14-21 in relation to the Book of the
        Prophet Joel. Note Peter's inclusion of the Gentiles in the fulfillment
        of Acts 2:39.
    3 - Is the valley of the judgment (Amos 3) a forecast of the last day?
        Compare this scene with Matthew 24:29-31: 25:31-46
    4 - Is this the Armageddon of the last days? Compare Revelation 16

We are in for prophetical treats as we move into the deeper histories of the divided
kingdom and the awesome words of the Prophets which ring with the awful judgment,
and yet resound with the grand and glorious promises of the NEW KINGDOM to come.

****

BIBLE READING GUIDE
    for BIBLE READING PEOPLE

June 5 (Israel) (no reading)	June 5 - 814 B.C. II Chronicles 24:23-27 II Kings 12:17-21 Enemies from the outside - Conspiracy within
June 6 II Kings 13:14-25 Strange prophecy from a dying prophet	June 6 II Chronicles 25:1-5; II Kings 14:1-6 A good life and a good king for 29 years
June 7 (no reading)	June 7 802 B.C. II Kings 14:7; II Chronicles 25:6-13 The power of God is mightier than the power of mercenary men
June 8 (no reading)	June 8 II Chronicles 25:14-16 Idolatry makes God angry
June 9 II Kings 14:8-14 Israel conquers Judah	June 9 II Chronicles 25:17-24 North wins -- South is conquered
June 10 II Kings 13:12-13; 14:15-16 The end of another reign "He slept with his fathers"	June 10 799 B.C. II Chronicles 25:25; 26:1-5 II Kings 14:17 & 21-22; 15:1-4 "God made him prosper"
June 11 II Kings 14:23-27 Forty-one BAD years - But - Saved in spite of it	June 11 II Kings 14:18-20; II Chron. 25:26-28 Conspiracy against the King

REFLECTIONS ON READINGS

June 5 through June 11

1 - II Chron. 24:17ff. - The people's failure to heed - Do we fail to heed? Discuss
    II Chron. 25:15ff. - The prophet's warnings: "When you don't like the message,
    kill the messenger". -- In church, - "too-yet"!
    God's anger is voiced through the prophet
    How do you think God shows his anger in today's world?

2 - II Chron. 24:23-27 - What the mercy of God means toward protection
    II Kings 13:14ff. - ONLY GOD HAS THE POWER!
    II Chron. 25:6ff. - God intervenes -- The "weaker" army wins
    Does this reflect in power struggles in nations today? How?

3 - II Kings 14:3ff   - Amaziah succeeds Joash in Judah - 800 B.C - mixed blessings
    Challenges Israel -- Some good diplomacy fails --
    Judah goes down in defeat.

4 - II Chron. 26:15   - Uzziah succeeds Amaziah in Judah. Mixed blessings--
    Has a religious advisor.

    II Chron. 26:15   - Invention of arrows and stone throwers, but Uzziah was
    powerful because of the help he got from God.

****

BIBLE READING GUIDE
for BIBLE READING PEOPLE

June 12   774 B.C. (Israel)
Amos 9:11-15: Hosea 1:1-11
Read New Testament - Acts 15:15-21
FUTURE RESTORATION PROMISED

June 12   (Judah)
II Chronicles 26:6-15
A good reputation with God's help

June 13
Hosea 2:1-23
Law and Gospel in romantic terms

June 13 to June 30
(No readings in reference to the
Southern Kingdom)

June 14 - Hosea 3:1-5

Adulterous people --
Still loved by God

June 15 - Jonah 1:1-17 (767 B.C.)

SPECIAL PROPHET --SPECIAL MISSION

June 16 - Jonah 2:1-10

A special way to get him to obey!

(JOKE!! "How did Jonah feel when swallowed by the whale?

Answer: "A little down in the mouth" --

June 17 - Jonah 3

The Message and the MIRACLE

June 18 - Jonah 4

A man's madness --
and GOD'S MERCY

June 12 through June 18

The message from the Prophet Hosea:
    Note the corollary of Amos 9:11-15 in the New Testament Book of Acts 15:1ff,
    especially vs. 15-18.

Pictures of the national circumstances depicted through an unfaithful marriage --
    Compare Hosea 2:18-23 with Romans 9:22ff. and I Peter 2:10.

The message and the miracle of Jonah:
    Discuss - What is the real message of Jonah?
                How and is what ways do we as individuals, the church, and nation
                seek "to go in the other direction"?
                How and in what way has the Lord turned you around?
                Compare Jonah with Jesus -- (Jonah 1:5-6 & Matthew 8:23-25; 12:39-42

The real message of Jonah is not just power over creation - obviously God has that
    -- all the time -- not just sustenance of life -- God has that all the
    time. too. God is truly omni-scient; omni-present; omni-powerful--all the time!

The real message: REPENTANCE AND REDEMPTION by DEATH AND RESURRECTION --
                Self-sacrifice for the deliverance of others. (Jonah 1:12)

Preach God's message and enjoy it!   (Jonah 4:1)

****

BIBLE READING GUIDE
        for BIBLE READING PEOPLE

June 19 - Amos 1:1-15   764 B.C.   A farmers fearful message of doom
                                          for God's enemies

June 20 - Amos 2:1-16   A fearful message of doom for
                                          God's own people

June 21 - Amos 3:1-15   God's special secrets
                                          given to special prophets

June 22 - Amos 4:1-13   The people refuse to hear
                                          the Prophet -- SO?

June 23 - Amos 5:1-27   A call to return and to repent

June 24 - Amos 6:1-27   Feasts and banquets will come
                                          to an end

June 25 - Amos 7:1-9   The Prophet pleads for the people

<u>REFLECTIONS ON READINGS</u>

June 19 through June 25

The heavy message of <u>AMOS</u>!

Consider the conflict between the priest and the prophet -- Amos 7:10-13

    Discuss: What are the contemporary lessons for us to learn from a
          Book like Amos?

    Consider again: What are the future restoration plans?
                Study that comparison again - Amos 9:11-15 with Acts 15:15-18

****

<u>BIBLE READING GUIDE</u>
    <u>for BIBLE READING PEOPLE</u>

June 26 - Amos 7:10-17	The <u>Prophet</u> pricks the the politician King
June 27 - Amos 8:1-14	Songs of the Temple turn to sadness and trembling
June 28 - Amos 9:1-10 (Review 9:11-15)	Judgments of God turned to grace and glory
June 29 - II Kings 14:28-29 762 B.C.	Meanwhile — Back at the Kingdom
June 30 - Hosea 4:1-19	Even the priests fall prey to priestly sins
<u>July 1</u> ISRAEL 762 B.C. II Kings 15:1-19 The bad gets even worse	<u>July 1</u> JUDAH (no reading)
<u>July 2</u> 751 B.C. II Kings 15:19-24 Bribes really don't pay	<u>July 2</u> 754 B.C. II Chronicles 26:16-23 Kings and Priest in conflict

****

<u>REFLECTIONS ON READINGS</u>

June 26 through July 2

The closing readings on Amos were included in the previous week's <u>Reflections</u>.

After assessing the message of the three Prophets, Hosea (3 chapters), Jonah, and Amos, the readings this week take us back to the chronological sequence of the happenings of the divided kingdom, Israel and Judah.

II Kings 15:13ff - <u>Shallum</u> rules for one month and dies by assassination.
<u>Menahem</u>, a vicious despot, rules for 10 years. II Kings 15:16
<u>Uzziah</u>, (called Azariah in some texts) trangresses the priestly
rites and suffers for it.   II Chronicles 26:16-21

II Kings 15:19-24 - <u>Pekahiah</u> succeeds Menahem, rules for two years and is
assassinated

****

<u>BIBLE READING GUIDE</u>
<u>for BIBLE READING PEOPLE</u>

<u>ASSYRIA BECOMES THE WORLD POWER</u>

<u>July 3</u> (Israel)
II Kings 15:25-28
More evil in the sight of the Lord

<u>July 3</u> (Judah) 748 B.C.
Isaiah 6:1-13
A grand vision from God

<u>July 4</u>
(no reading)

<u>July 4</u>
II Chronicles 27:1-2;II Kings 15:32-35
A trend to the righteous

<u>July 5</u>
(no reading)

<u>July 5</u>
Isaiah 1:1; 2:1-5
Great visions from the Spirit

<u>July 6</u>
(no reading)

<u>July 6</u>
Isaiah 2:6-22
Chastisement comes before blessing

<u>July 7</u>
(no reading)

<u>July 7</u>
Isaiah 3:1-26
Predictions of the downfall of Judah

<u>July 8</u>
(no reading)

<u>July 8</u>
Isaiah 4:1-6; 5:1-7
A vision of the future glory

<u>July 9</u>
(no reading)

<u>July 9</u>
Isaiah 5:8-13   The woes of the
ungrateful, affluent society

****

<u>REFLECTIONS ON READINGS</u>

July 3 through July 9

<u>Pekah</u> becomes king of Israel (Northern Kingdom) - II Kings 15:27
TIGLATH-PILEZER (Assyrian) invades northern cities and takes the first wave of
the Israelites captive to Assyria.

The great Book of the Prophet Isaiah details the lives of four kings:
UZZIAH, JOTHAM, AHAZ, AND HEZEKIAH -- 96 years -- 783-687B.C.

THE GREAT THEMES OF ISAIAH

JUSTICE and JOY

Interesting verses and chapters
Justice and justification: 1:17-21
The Love Song: 5:1
Sin forgiven: 6:7; 32:24; 40:2 64:9
DO NOT FEAR: 7:4; 37:6; 41:10; 43;1; 51:7
A precious child: 9:6
Stump of Jesse: 11:1
Compassion: 14:1
Defender - Deliverer: 19:20
Perfect peace: 46:2; 48:18; 55:12
Comfort: 40:1
Shepherd   40:11
Belonging to God
and His Abiding Presence: 43:1
Beautiful feet   52:7; (Rf.Romans 10:14ff)
Vicarious Suffering Chap. 53
Everlasting Love/Abundant life: Chap 55
Call and Invitation: 55:6
Call to the Nations: Chap.60
New Heaven and New Earth 65:17

Interesting Concepts
Joy & Singing: 14:7; 24:14-15; 25:9
                 26:1ff; 29:19; 30:29
                 35:10; 40:9-10; 44:23
                 51:11
The Remnant: 4:3;46:3;63:3;64:5;66:10
            (See Hebrews 3:10ff)
God's Wrath: 2:24; 9:19; 34:8; 35:4;
             47:3 & 6; 57:17
JUSTICE: 9:7; 16:3-5; 32:16; 42:1,3,4;
         56:1; 59:8,9,11,14,15; 61:8
IMMANUEL: 7:14
Salvation: 12:2; 62:11
Potter/Clay: 45:9; 64:8
Overconfidence in overkill: 30:15-17
No other God:48:12
Fasting: Chap.58

ALL WORSHIP 66:23

****

A brief return to righteousness: II Chronicles 27:1-2; II Kings 15

As you read Isaiah, make an attempt to discern between the historic, the prophetic,
and the apocalyptic in the message. Give attention to the combinations.

As you read, think on the application to society and nations today.

Give special interest and attention to LAW/GOSPEL and JUDGMENT/MERCY themes.

****

BIBLE READING GUIDE
for BIBLE READING PEOPLE

July 10 (Israel)
(no reading)

July 10 (Judah) 744 B.C.
Micah 1:1-16 -- God's displeasure
declared through a prophet

July 11
(no reading)

July 11
Micah 2:1-13; II Chronicles 27:3-6
It is darkest -- just before the dawn

July 12
(no reading)

July 12
II Kings 15:36-37; 16:1-4;
II Chronicles 27:7-9; 28:1-4
GOOD NEWS -- BAD NEWS

July 13 (Israel) 732 B.C.   July 13 (Judah)

          II Chronicles 28:5-8
     The Northern Kingdom subdues the South

July 14   July 14
(no reading)   Isaiah 7:10-16; 9:1-7
                                             A great sign for the future

July 15   July 15
(no reading)   Isaiah 7:17-25; 8:5-22
                                             Predictions of invasion

July 16   July 16
(no reading)   Isaiah 9:8-21; 10:1-4
                                             A Word of chastisement to North & South

****

REFLECTIONS ON READINGS

July 10 through July 16

Introduction to Micah, contemporary of Isaiah, Messenger to the Southern Kingdom
       Awful messages of judgment: Chapter 1, vs. 3
       Resistance to the prophet: Chapter 2
       The hope of ingathering: Chapter 2,12-13

Back to Historical sequence;
       God's role in the decision of war -- II Kings 15:37; II Chronicles 28:5-6
       The incredible sacrifice of a son -- II Kings 16:3
       Contrasting regimes: Ahaz & Jotham - II Chronicles 27:6; 28:1ff
       The Lord's signal
       An interesting study on the psychosis of war - II Chronicles 8:5-15

The great MESSIANIC VISIONS of Isaiah --- Isaiah 7:10-16; 9:1-7
       The immediate and the futuristic event: (see Matthew 1)
       Compare Isaiah 9 with Luke 1:29ff; Luke 1:54-55; Luke 1:76ff; Luke 2:29ff
       Compare Isaiah 61:1-3 with Luke 4:16ff.

****

BIBLE READING GUIDE
for BIBLE READING PEOPLE

July 17   July 17
     II Chronicles 28:9-15; II Kings 16:5-6; Isaiah 7:1-2

THE CHRONICLES AND TRAGEDIES OF CIVIL WAR

July 18   July 18
(no reading)   Isaiah 7:3-9; II Chronicles 28:16-21

July 19   July 19
(no reading)   Psalm 50
                                             God speaks of HOPE: - and HELL!

July 20
(no reading)

July 20
Isaiah 8:1-4; 17:1-14; Destruction
prevails on the self-powered people

July 21
(no reading)

July 21
II Kings 16:7-9
The enemy collides with itself

July 22
II Kings 15:29; I Chron.5:25-26
Northern heathen powers invade

July 22
Isaiah 1:2-31
The warnings of judgment

July 23
(no reading

July 23
II Kings 16:10-18
Holy people turn to pagan acts

****

REFLECTIONS ON READINGS

July 17 through July 23

Reflect, again, on the Messianic Visions of July 14 - (Last week's REFLECTIONS)

A tremendous message of confidence: Isaiah 8:9-22

WORDS FULL OF WARNING: Isaiah 9:8-21; 10:1-4

A little known prophet (Obed) has an important word - II Chronicles 28:9ff.

A New Testament message in Old Testament context --- Isaiah 9b

A Psalm reflection of LAW/GOSPEL - the awesome judgment scene: Psalm 50:1-6; 15-23;
     Compare with Matthew 23:29ff and Matthew 25:11

A comment on obedience -- Psalm 50:23
     The first step in obedience is to believe in God's mercy in Christ for
     salvation. Without that, all other obedience avails nothing at all with God.
     See John 8:24; 51; 12:47

Words of Israel's doom: Isaiah 1:2-31
     The Gospel set in the warning words of judgment: Isaiah 17:1-20 & vs.27

Worship must be true, not sacrilege: II Kings 16:10ff

****

BIBLE READING GUIDE
for BIBLE READING PEOPLE

July 24   729 B.C.
II Kings 15:30-31; 17:1-2
Unrest and conspiracy

July 24
II Chronicles 28:22-27 - Distress and
trespass often go hand in hand

July 25 (Israel)	July 25 (Judah)
Isaiah 28:1-8	II Kings 18:1-8; II Chronicles 29:1-2
Woe to the fat and to the proud	A late revival restores hope.

July 26	July 26
Isaiah 28:9-29 - Judgment followed	II Chronicles 29:3-19
by great measures of mercy	Revival and reconstruction

July 27	July 27
Hosea 5:5-15 -- Desolation dwells	II Chronicles 29:20-30 - The grand
in the land of the unrighteous	noise of worship fills the air

July 28	July 28
Hosea 6:1-11	II Chronicles 29:31-36
A call to repent	Too few priests to praise God

July 29 725 B.C.	July 29
	II Chronicles 30:1-6

REUNION AND RECONCILIATION BRING GREAT JOY

July 30   July 30

Psalm 81
PRAISE GOD FROM WHOM ALL BLESSINGS FLOW

July 31	July 31
II Chronicles 31:1	II Kings 18:4
Idols thrown out	Nehushtan (look it uup!

****

REFLECTIONS ON READINGS

July 24 through July 31

Human nature caves in: Betrays the Lord Almighty -- II Chronicles 28:22ff.

The revival of righteousness in Judah ------   II Kings 18:1-6

A sad day of debauchery, -- But great measures of mercy: -- Isaiah 28:1-8

Compare Isaiah 28:16-17 with Ephesian 2:19-22; I Corinthians 3:10-16; I Pet.2:4-8

The importance of the TEMPLE in worship: ----   II Chronicles 29:3

Isn't worship exciting?? --------------------   II Chronicles 29:20-30

Reinstitution of the sacred Passover- II Chronicles 30:1: When did you last share
                                                     the Holy Meal?

On the other side of the track - (Northern Kingdom) - Hosea 5 & 6

A Closing Psalm -- 81   PRAISE GOD FROM ALL WHOM ALL BLESSINGS FLOW

BIBLE READING GUIDE
     for BIBLE READING PEOPLE

August 1 (Israel)   August 1 (Judah) 725 B.C.
(no reading)   II Chronicles 31:2-21
                                     WORSHIP with ALL you've got

August 2   August 2
(no reading)   Micah 3:1-12
                                     Full of power by the Spirit

August 3   August 3
II Kings 17:3-4; Hosea 7:1-16   (no reading)
Bottles of wine, but no Spirit

August 4   August 4
Hosea 8:1-14   (no reading)
Israel forgot its Maker

August 5   August 5
Hosea 9:1-17 - The Day of   (no reading)
Reckoning is a harsh day indeed

August 6   August 6
Hosea 10:1-15   (no reading)
Divided heart and spirit

August 7   August 7
Hosea 11:1-12   (no reading)
Bent to Backsliding

****

REFLECTIONS ON READINGS

August 1 through August 7

One great important word -- JUSTICE -- Micah Chapter 3

One whole hour with one prophet -- HOSEA

Review Reflections of June 12 - 18

     Outline of Hosea:

          I - Hosea's marriage and family   1:1 - 3:5

          II - Messages against Israel ----- 4:1 -13:16
               The wine flows but the Spirit is lacking - 7:5ff
               Claiming to believe but rejecting the essential -- 8:2
               No offering for the Lord   --   9:4
               Justice and injustice--War and Peace 10:4 & 12ff.

          III - The turmoil in the heart of God -- Chapter 11

A contemporary corollary of the message of Hosea:

   Quotes from an article in the July 31, Sunday Mississippi Press,Pascagoula,Ms.
   Article written by Vivian Austin, reviewing the NAACP Rally at Gautier, Ms.
   Junior College - July 1983.

   "Most importantly, I went to the rally on Thursday because I believe in
Almighty God and his Son, Jesus Christ. And I believe God was tired of hearing his
people crying from oppression and the sin of prejudice and he looked down from
heaven and had pity. In the name of Jesus, he answered the prayers of my parents,
grandparents, and ancestors before them.
   "I was glad to hear everyone of the speakers give honor to God as the One who
brought the black race out of the wilderness and put us on the road to the promised
land. It was not by accident that Dr. Martin Luther King, Jr. was a pastor. If
blacks will look back they will see that every leader who has been truly a great
leader for the black community has been a man filled with the Spirit of God. And
anyone supposing to make any kind of move with blacks without including the church's
backing is making a grave mistake.

A LOT OF THINGS HAVE CHANGED IN 20 YEARS

   "Some things changed for the worst. Let's face it, people. Some of us took
what was a holy blessing from God and threw it to the dogs.
   "God took us out of the shacks and shanties and put us in brick homes with
running water, lights, heaters and air conditioners. Instead of putting in prayer
rooms where we could get on our knees and thank Him, we installed bars and filled
them with Scotch, Brandy and Whiskey to drunken our minds to the goodness bestowed on
us and to make us forget how we got those blessings.
   "God gave us food stamps to feed our children and each other so we wouldn't
have to subsist on diets of milk and bread with fatback and still expect our bodies
to function properly during a day of hard work. Instead of feeding the hungry still
around us and teaching our children how to take care of 'God's temples', we
furnished food to 'party hardy' with beer money we then didn't have to buy food."

****

BIBLE READING GUIDE
   for BIBLE READING PEOPLE

August 8 (Israel)
Hosea 12:1-14
Wait on God continually

August 9
Hosea 13:1-8
Sinning more and more

August 10
Hosea 13:9-16
Self-destroyed -- Spirit Renewed

August 11
Hosea 14:1-9
The ways of the Lord are RIGHT!

August 8 (Judah)
(no reading)

August 9
(no reading)

August 10
(no reading)

August 11
(no reading)

August 12 II Kings 17:5-23; 18:9-12	August 12 (no reading)
August 13 Psalm 80 Come now, and save us	August 13 (no reading)
August 14 II Kings 16:19-20; II Chron. 28:26 ISRAEL'S FALL COMES FIRST	August 14 Isaiah 21:1-17; JUDAH'S FALL FOLLOWS

****

REFLECTIONS ON READINGS

August 8 through August 14

Reflect on Hosea 12:2-6 -- A span of history that covers 1000 years. (1710 - 721B.C.

An Old Testament/New Testament comparison -- Hosea 12:10ff with Hebrews 1.

How final is the Word of Judgment -- Hosea 13

How promising the Word of grace ---- Hosea 14
      Compare Mark 1:14-15; 3:28; 6:4; 7:6ff; 13:9-10 & 34ff; 15:9
          Luke 13:14; Luke 19:9-10; John 18;36-38

The struggle against Jesus was waged by Jews and Gentiles alike -- Acts 4:27

The New Kingdom includes the Jews who seek forgiveness: (Hosea 14 - Acts 5:31)
      AND the Gentiles -- Acts 8:26ff; 10:45; Romans 4:11
      Check the following verses concerning Jew/Gentile relationship
          Romans 9:1-8 & 24; 11:1-12; I Corinthians 3:11; Galatians 3:7

Israel's final day - (Northern Kingdom) - II Kings 17:5-23: (723-721 B.C.)

In this setting, read Psalm 80 -- A Prayer for national restoration

****

BIBLE READING GUIDE
for BIBLE READING PEOPLE

August 15 - Judgment and destruction on the unrighteous -- 713 B.C.	Isaiah 14:28-32; 15:1-9
16 - A small and feeble remnant shall remain	Isaiah 16:1-14
17 - A time of prospering before the fall	II Kings 18:7-8; I Chronicles 4:39-43; Isaiah 18:1-7
18 - Egypt also has her turn for judgment	Isaiah 19:1-25; 20:1-6

August 19 – THE JOY IS ALL GONE!   Isaiah 23:1-18; 10:5-19

      20 – The REMNANT remains   Isaiah 10:20-34; 11:1-16

ISRAEL (NORTHERN KINGDOM) IN EXILE

jUDAH (SOUTHERN KINGDOM) SURVIVES

720 B.C. to 585 B.C.

****

REFLECTIONS ON READINGS

August 15 through 20

"Isaiah hath foretold it" -- Messianic Prophecy -- Isaiah 21:1-17
Pertains also to the judgment prophecy -- That dare not be overlooked

Consider these "Babylon" concepts:

    Consider the fall of Babylon as described in Revelation 18
    Compare Matthew 3:9; 23:37ff; Isaiah 22:14

    As "Old" Israel becomes "New" Israel (spiritualized)
    So "Old" Babylon becomes a "New" Babylon (spiritualized)
    The whole world, except for those who have come in to the Kingdom,
    ("The New Israel") is BABYLON.

    As Israelites of old (Old Israel) were promised escape from Old Babylon,
    to return to Palestine
    So the New Israel (New Testament Kingdom of God) is promised escape from
    worldly Babylon to the eternal Kingdom of Glory which is heaven.

Discuss: -- Luther's concept of the separate distinctions of the
             Kingdom of power -- the Kingdom of grace -- and the Kingdom of Glory

    The beginnings of the Shepherd theme: Isaiah 14:30 -- Compare John 10
    Other Shepherd pictures to refer to: I Peter 2:24-25; 5:4; Hebrews 13:20

    A beautiful Messianic segment: Isaiah 16:5
    Compare Isaiah 18 with Hebrews 12:22

    The presence of God's Gospel in Egypt - St. Augustine - early patriarch
    The Christian Society in Egypt today -- The Coptics - Isaiah 19:20

    Fire from the throne -- Isaiah 10:16-19 -- (Nuclear Devastation?)

    THE REMNANT BEGINS: Isaiah 10:20ff -- Compare Romans 9:6 and 30ff.

August 21 - Joy and judgment   Isaiah 12:1-5; 13:1-22

        22 - Re-possessing a lost land   Isaiah 14:1-27

        23 - I believe in God Almighty --   Isaiah 24:1-23
             SHAKER of Heaven and earth   713 B.C.

        24 - This is the Lord - we waited   Isaiah 25:1-12; 26:1-21
             for Him and REJOICED

        25 - Valleys full of chariots   Isaiah 27:1-13; 22:1-14; 34:1-17

        26 - Hezekiah's heavy heart -   Isaiah 35:1-10; II Kings 20:1-11;
             and HEALING   II Chronicles 32:24-26

        27 - Recovery brings rejoicing   Isaiah 38:1-22

****

REFLECTIONS ON READINGS

August 21 through August 27

Discuss: -- WHO IS ISRAEL?
        Romans 9:6ff -- translated literally from the Greek:
        "Not however that has failed the Word (Logos) of God; for not all those
        which are of Israel, those of Israel are."
    Compare Isaiah 11 with Luke 2:40; 4:18ff; John 3:34-16; Matthew 12:17-21;21:4ff
        Matthew 28:19ff
    An interesting sidelight -- Job 14:7-9
        We've got to get the BIG PICTURE
        The culminating glory - Revelation 5:5; 22:16
    Compare: Isaiah 11:4 with II Thessalonians 2:18-17
              Isaiah 11:10 with Romans 15:7ff.

Isaiah 12 - A beautiful hymn for the Old and the New Israel -- Also Isaiah 26

    Compare: Isaiah 24:14 with Matthew 25:31; Revelation 5:11; 7:9; 21:12ff.
              Isaiah 24:21-23 with Romans 8:37ff; Ephesians 6:10ff.
              Isaiah 25:6 with Revelation 19:5ff; Matthew 22:1-14

RESURRECTION TIME: Isaiah 26:19; Isaiah 27:1; Compare Is.26:21 with Revelation 21:8

    References (11) in Revelation to the dragon: Revelation 12:3ff; 13:2ff; 16:13ff
    Compare: Isaiah 27:13 with Revelation 10:5-7
              Isaiah 34:4 with Matthew 24:29; Mark 13:24; Luke 21:25ff;
                                Hebrews 1:10ff; and Revelation 6:13-14
              Isaiah 34:10 with Revelation 14:11; 19:3; also Mark 9:44-45

Back to reality: - Isaiah and King Hezekiah: - II Kings 20; II Chronicles 32:24;26

A Beautiful song of praise for recovery from illness -- Isaiah 38:10-20

BIBLE READING GUIDE
    for BIBLE READING PEOPLE

August   28 - A great word of comfort   Isaiah 40:1-31; 41:1-29

          29 - Restoration and redemption   Isaiah 42:1-23; 43:1-28

          30 - A fervent witness -   Isaiah 44:1-27
               to the glory of God

          31 - King Cyrus - a prototype   Isaiah 45:1-25; 46:1-13; 47:1-15
               of the coming Christ

September 1 - The difference between   Isaiah 48:1-22
               what we pretend to be and
               what God knows we are

           2 - God's mission - Restoration - Isaiah 49:1-26
               -The Messiah Complex-

           3 - The WORD in season --   Isaiah 50:1-11
               Strengthens the weary

****

REFLECTIONS ON READINGS

August 28 through September 3

Prophetic Messianic Messages -- With fulfillment

          Isaiah 40   ----- Matthew 3:2-12; Luke 1:17
          Isaiah 40:8   ---   John 1:1-14; Hebrew 13:8
          Isaiah 40:10-11 -   The Messianic lines of Handel's "MESSIAH"

What a Revelation! - What an incomparable God! (Isaiah 40:12ff)

The most recurrent theme in Scripture - "Don't be Afraid" -- Isaiah 41:10 & 14;
          Culminating with the angel's message -- Luke 2:10; Matthew 28:10

MOOD CHANGE: More HOPE - More COMFORT - Note the past tense -- Isaiah 42:23ff
          "Called by Name" - Isaiah 43; Hebrews 12:23; Revelation 3:11ff

     Note the recurrence of the court scene -- Isaiah 41:1 & 21; 43:8
          Compare Isaiah 43:10 with Acts 1:8

     LAW & GOSPEL in precise forms -- Isaiah 43:22-28

A PICTURE OF THE NEW ISRAEL IN THE OLD TESTAMENT: -- Isaiah 44:5
          Cyrus and the restoration -- A prototype of the Delivering Christ to come
     Compare Isaiah 45:22ff with Philippians 2:1-11 and Matthew 25:31ff.
               Isaiah 46:2ff with Luke 1:67 and Luke 2:29ff

     A Question: -- Consider Isaiah 49:8ff -- Is it historical or contemporary?

September 4 - God's greatness   Isaiah 51:1-23; 52:1-15
                encourages the faithful

          5 - A little WRATH -   Isaiah 53:1-12; 54:1-17
                A lot of MERCY

          6 - Everybody COME   Isaiah 55:1-13; 56:1-12

          7 - To worship is to do JUSTICE   Isaiah 57:1-21; 58:1-14
                and care for the POOR

          8 - Sins separate --   Isaiah 59:1-21; 60:1-22
                The REDEEMER unites

          9 - How beautiful the Spirit   Isaiah 61:1-11; 62:1-12
                                                  Luke 4:16-21

         10 - God's vengeance relieved   Isaiah 63:1-19; 64:1-12
                by a prayer of intercession

****

REFLECTIONS ON READINGS

September 4 through September 10

A look back -- Isaiah 51;1-2; 9-10 -- Compare Genesis 12:3
A look ahead - Isaiah 51;3ff
            Consider the interpretive problem:
            Is it historic -- Messianic -- apocalyptic -- or eschatological?
    Compare: Isaiah 52:7 with Romans 10:15
            Isaiah 53:6 with II Corinthians 5:21
            Isaiah 53:10 with Colossians 2:13ff

Apply the above interpretive question to Isaiah 52

Discuss the Old Testament picture of the dying Jesus -- Isaiah 53
        Discuss Isaiah 53 with its LAW/GOSPEL applications
        Do the same with Isaiah 54

Discuss and share the "Gospel Call" of Isaiah 55

Lessons on evangelism: Jews to Gentiles -- Old Testament style -- Isaiah 56
                       Gentiles to Jews -- New Testament style -- Romans 10:1ff

The folly of religious ceremony without social concern --Discuss Isaiah 57 & 58
        Compaare with Amos 5 & 2 -- Review Isaiah 1:18-20

Study again the concepts of Isiah 60: Is it literal or symbolic
        Again: Is it Messianic - eschatologic - historical - apocalyptic?
        Compare this chapter with Revelation 21
        Are verses 6 & 7 prophetic of the wise men coming to Jesus? Matt. 2

Compare: Isaiah 61 with Luke 4:15ff;   Isaiah 61:10 with Revelation 18:7ff

What's in a name? Consider the beautiful NEW NAMES -- Isaiah 62

Compare: The new names of Isaiah with the names in Revelation 2:17 & 3:12

When all the chips are down -- How does God save? --
        Through Law? --- Isaiah 63:1-6; -- See also Hebrews 3:10ff. OR
        Through Gospel? - Isaiah 63:7ff; 64:6-9

****

BIBLE READING GUIDE
    for BIBLE READING PEOPLE

September 11 - A new world of JOY out of   Isaiah 65:1-25
               an old world of sadness

        12 - REJOICE and be glad   Isaiah 66:1-24

        13 - The future Kingdom --   Micah 4:1-13
             What's it like?   (704 B.C.)

        14 - God's displeasure is   Micah 5:1-15; 6:1-16
             overruled by His PARDON

        15 - Where is there a God --   Micah 7:1-20; II Chronicles 32:1;
             Like OUR God?   Isaiah 36:1;   II Kings 18:13-16

        16 - The right alliance with God   II Chronicles 32:2-14; Isaiah 36:2-11
             more important than   II Kings 18:17-26
             a strong army

        17 - The false prophet faces off   II Kings 18:27-35; Isaiah 36:12-20
             with the faithful   II Chronicles 32:15-19

****

REFLECTIONS ON READINGS

September 11 through September 17

A JOYFUL JERUSALEM: -- Isaiah 65:17ff -- Compare Revelation 21:1ff

    Again -- Is it historic? -- Literal? -- Figurative? -- Symbolic?
            Messianic? -- Apocalyptic? -- Eschatalogic?

    Consider Isaiah 66 in that same light
            Discuss your impressions, feelings, and your opinions of Isaiah
            the Prophet and the words that God inspired him to write.

MICAH -- <u>THE MESSAGE AND THE MAN</u>

       Apply the questions of reflection pertaining to Isaiah 65 to the remaining
       chapter of Micah - (4,5,6,& 7). Refresh your thoughts on Micah from
       reflections of July 17 through 23.

       Considered the most precise and specific of all prophecies pertaining to the
       coming of Christ. Compare Micah 5:2 with Matthew 2:5

Back to the historic reality: King Hezekiah and the invading Sennacherib --
       Review II Kings 18:13ff; II Chronicles 32:1ff; Isaiah 36
       Note the similarity of these historic accounts.

****

<u>BIBLE READING GUIDE</u>
    <u>for BIBLE READING PEOPLE</u>

September 18 - Get tough in the faith   Isaiah 29:1-24

        19 - Alliances with nations   Isaiah 30:1-33
             without the right alliance
             with God leads to no where

        20 - Worries give way   Isaiah 31:1-9; 32:1-20
             to a wonderful trust

        21 - Woes to the spoiler --   Isaiah 33:1-27; II Kings 18:36-37
             praise to the Lord!

        22 - A Prophet gives some good   Isaiah 36:21-22; 37:1-7
             advice to a Prince   II Kings 19:1-7; Psalm 44

        23 - In time of trouble --   Psalm 2;
             consult the Lord   II Kings 19:8-19; Isaiah 37:8-20

        24 - Only the Remnant   Psalm 73:1-28; II Kings 19:20-34
             will remain   Isaiah 37:21-38

****

<u>REFLECTIONS ON READINGS</u>

September 18 through September 24

A few more thoughts from your review of Isaiah:

       Read Isaiah 29 through the microscopic vision of LAW/GOSPEL analyses
       Read Isaiah 30 with a contemporary view of what nations, (and the church)
          are like today.
          Apply the same question to Isaiah 31,32,33

The ultimate glory of God and His People:
       Compare Isaiah 33:17-24 with Revelation 21:1-7

Consider: - Do politics and religion mix?
　　　　　Discuss the relationship between the Prophet and the Prince - Isaiah 37

Psalm 44 -- A beautiful prayer for protection in disturbing times
　　　　Compare Psalm 2 with Isaiah 37:21ff.

Review the concept of the REMNANT once again -
　　　　Isaiah 37:32; II Kings 19:31; Psalm 78

****

BIBLE READING GUIDE
　　　for BIBLE READING PEOPLE

September 25 - Man's might cut down by Angel's power	II Kings 19:35-36 II Chronicles 32:20-22
26 - Judgment turns to joy and prosperity	Psalm 75:1-10; 76:1-12; II Chronicles 32:23-30
27 - A prophecy of disaster	II Kings 20:12-21; Isaiah 39:1-8 II Chronicles 32:31-33
28 - The take-over (697-642B.C.)	II Kings 17:24-41
29 - A leader leading people -	II Kings 21:1-16; II Chronicles 33:1-9
30 - After much trouble -- Some thanksgiving (674 B.C.)	Isaiah 22:15-22; II Kings 19:37 II Chronicles 33:10-17
October 1 - Good and bad in the leadership of the Kingdom	II Kings 21:17-26; 22:1-2; 23:25; II Chronicles 33:18-25

****

REFLECTIONS ON READINGS

September 25 through October 1

Prophecy fulfilled in Sennacherib's death -- II Kings 19:35-36

Times of peace and joy -- A beautiful breathing spell!
　　　II Kings 20:12ff; II Chronicles 32:23-30; Psalm 75 & 76

　　　Recall and discuss times of war and peace in our own country
　　　　　Why the recurring cycles of war in the world?
　　　　　Do you think it's possible for "everlasting peace on earth? --Discuss

Back to the doldrums -- exile -- confusion in worship -- II Kings 17:23-24

A new King -- but the same old disgusting practices under Manasseh
　　　II Kings 21:1-15; II Chronicles 33:1-9

WORSHIP AGAIN RESTORED
II Chronicles 33:15ff.

October 2 - A prophet's dread   Nahum 1:1-15; 2:1-13
            word of destruction

        3 - The corruption of a city   Nahum 3:1-19; II Chronicles 34:1-7
            leads to conflict

        4 - The call of a great prophet   Jeremiah 1:1-19

        5 - The prophets's powerful   Jeremiah 2:1-37
            message to backsliders

        6 - LIFT UP YOUR EYES   Jeremiah 3:1-5

        7 - God's day of wrath is an   Zephaniah 1:1-18; 2:1-14
            AWE-ful, awful day

        8 - A time of restoration   Zephaniah 3:1-20: II Kings 22:3-7
            and rejoicing   II Chronicles 34:8-13

****

REFLECTIONS ON READINGS

October 2 through October 8

NAHUM (635 B.C.) -- Another prophet on the scene --

    About the city of Ninevah:
        Review the "Reflections" on Jonah -- June 12-18 -- (767 B.C.)

    Discuss the movement and spirit of cities:
        Without God -- with God -- Without God!
        A breathing of hatred and vengeance

    There is little GOSPEL in Nahum:
        Exception? Note 1:7 & 15;   Compare Romans 10:14-18

THANK GOD FOR THE FAITHFUL:
    Josiah - King of Judah - establishes true worship
                            abolishes the pagan altars -- II Chronicles 34:3-7

THE GREAT PROPHET JEREMIAH -- Jeremiah 1:1-19 -- 627 B.C.

    Look for parallels and differences with Isaiah
    Messenger to Judah -- Southern Kingdom
    Josiah, Jehoiakim and Zedekiah -- The last of the breed (Kings of Judah)
        A span of 50 years at the end of Judah's independance
    The people of Jerusalem move into exile -- Jeremiah 1:2
    The awesome challenge --(visions) --------- Jeremiah 1:14ff

ZEPHANIAH -- Another prophet of awesome judgment -- Chapter 1 & 2 -- 628 B.C.

October 9 - They found the WORD --   II Kings 22:8-20
              and they READ IT!   II Chronicles 34:14-28

        10 - The WORD is sometimes   II Kings 23:1-3; Jeremiah 3:6-25
             a devastating WORD   II Chronicles 34;29-32

        11 - God hurts for the   Jeremiah 4:1-31
             foolishness of His people

        12 - The mixed emotion of God   Jeremiah 5:1-31
             concerning His people

        13 - The warnings of the Lord   Jeremiah 6:1-30
             are hard to contain

        14 - A remembrance of the Passover   II Kings 23:21-27; II Chron. 35:1-19

        15 - A day of recommitment   II Kings 23:4-20; II Chronicles 34:33

****

REFLECTIONS ON READINGS

October 9 through October 15

The continuation of awesome judgment (Law) -- Zephaniah 3:1-13
        Followed by a word of hope -- (Gospel)- Zephaniah 3:14-20
        Compare Zephaniah 3:8 with the judgment scene of Matthew 25:31-46
        Compare Zephaniah 3:9 with Philippians 2:9-11
        Put all that into the chronological setting of
                II Kings 22:3-7 and II Chronicles 34:8-13

THE LOST AND FOUND WORD OF GOD -- II Chronicles 34:8
        Compare with James 1:22; Luke 11:28; and II Timothy 3:14-17
        A woman prophet and her message -- II Chronicles 34:22ff.

Do we take our promises seriously? -- II Kings 23:1-3; II Chronicles 34:29-32

The image of marriage used as a symbol of the relationship of God with His people
        Jeremiah 3:6ff.

The Prophet's pain in the unfaithfulness of his people -- Jeremiah 4:19ff

Mixed emotions in the heart of God -- Jeremiah 5:1-31; 6:1-30

The importance of ceremony:
        Passover/Communion - II Kings 23:21ff; Matthew 26:17ff
        What an offering -- II Chronicles 35:1-14
        The sprinkling of blood -- Its significance
                Compare John 1:29ff; Hebrews 10:11-18; and I John 1:7
        How beautiful when the faithful return -- II Kings. 23 & II Chronicles 34

October 16 - Amend your way or away with you   Jeremiah 7:1-14

        17 - No balm for Gilead?   Jeremiah 8:1-22

        18 - A true spirit of humiliation   Jeremiah 9:1-26

        19 - Now hear the word of the Lord   Jeremiah 10:1-25

        20 - The word of promise   Jeremiah 11:1-23
             and the word of a curse

        21 - The spoilers have come --   Jeremiah 12:1-17
             But -- I WILL RETURN

        22 - BABYLON--THE WORLD POWER   II Kings 23:28-34
             (612 B.C. - 539 B.C.)   II Chronicles 35:20-27; 36:1-4

****

REFLECTIONS ON READINGS

October 16 through October 22

How seriously do we take the call to repentance? -- Jeremiah 7:1-34

Is there "Balm in Gilead" for us today? Explain -- Jeremiah 8:22

Discuss the evil things going on among God"s people? Are there similarities today?
    Compare Jeremiah 9 with Luke 23:27ff; and Matthew 11 :15-17; Luke 7:11ff
    In the midst of trouble -- a confident song -- Jeremiah 10
    The leading question of every generation --WHY? Jeremiah 12:1

The succession of the last kings:
    Josiah - 31 years; Jehoahaz (Joahaz) - 3 months; Jehoiachin - 11 years
            II Kings 23:28-34;   II Chronicles 35:20-27

BABYLON EMERGES AS THE WORLD POWER -- (612 - 539 B.C.)
            II Chronicles 36:6; Jeremiah 22:25-30

****

October 23 - Bonds and yokes   Jeremiah 22:10-12; 27:1-11
                                                 II Kings 23:35-36; II Chron. 36:5

        24 - Prophets are persecuted -   Jeremiah 26:1-20; Habakkuk 1:1-17
             even by God's people

        25 - God's promise   Habakkuk 2:1-20; 3:1-19
             brings prayer and praise

October 26	- No escape from the wrath of God	Jeremiah 35:1-19; 25:15-38
27	- The siege begins (606 B.C.)	Daniel 1:1-3; Jeremiah 25:1-11;36:1-8
28	- Total Disaster	Jeremiah 45:1-5;46:1-12;II Kings 24:7
29	- No compromise in the committed heart	Daniel 1:4-21; Jeremiah 22:13-19; 26:20-24

****

REFLECTIONS ON READING S

October 23 through October 29

A Prophet's message concerning the kings -- Jeremiah 22:10-18
        Cry for the right things -- Josiah (no) -- Joahaz (Yes) -- Jehoiachlin (no)

                Compare: Matthew 11:16-17; Luke 7:3; 23:28
                            Jeremiah 22:20-23 with Luke 21:20-24
                Parallels: Matthew 24:15-21 and Mark 13:14-19

Discus: --   The symbol of the yoke and Babylonian power -- Jeremiah 27:1-11

The importance of the words of the prophets:
        Action and violent reaction -- Jeremiah 26:1ff.
        God changes his mind -- Jeremiah 26: 13 & 19

HABAKKUK -- A minor prophet with a major message

                A GREAT BIG WHY -- 1:13
                        The Lord's answer -- Habakkuk 2:2
                        Habakkuk's response - Habakkuk 3
                        A mixture of disturbance and confidence
                        Compare I Thessalonians 1:6-10

A special promise to a special clan -- The Rechabites - Jeremiah 35
                A pietistic people founded in the time Jehu - 842 to 815 B.C.

JUDAH UNDER JUDGMENT -- along with all nations --
                An alarming message: - Jeremiah 36:16; 45:1-5

WARS OF OTHER NATIONS: - Jeremiah 46:1-12; II Kings 24:7
                Nebuchadnezzar (Babylon) defeats King Neco (Egypt)

Medicine for Gilead -- Jeremiah 46:11

Four great men of God -
                Their unique characteristics -- Daniel 1:4-20

October 30 - The meaning of a dream   Jeremiah 36:9; Daniel 2:1-49

    31 - The WORD --   Jeremiah 36:10-32
        Destroyed and restored

November 1 - The problem of pride   Jeremiah 13:1-27

    2 - The problem of prophets   Jeremiah 14:1-22
        prophesying lies

    3 - A REMNANT shall return   Jeremiah 15:1-21

    4 - In the midst of trouble --   Jeremiah 16:1-21
        a prayer of confidence

    5 - How deceitful the human heart   Jeremiah 17:1-27

****

REFLECTIONS ON READINGS

October 30 through November 5

What happened to the idea of fasting? -- Jeremiah 36:9
    What does Luther's Catechism say about fasting -- Question 320, page 203
    Compare: Matthew 6:16; Acts 13:2; 14:23; 27:33; I Corinthians 7:5;
        Also Colossians 2:16

The meaning of dreams?
    An interesting study in psychodynamics -- Daniel 2
    Visions that lead to the end of time -- Daniel 2:44

Alarming news from the word of the Lord -- Jeremiah 36:10ff.

A short story on shorts -- and its meaning -- Jeremiah 13:1-11
                 and wine jars -- 13:2

The problem of false prophets -- Jeremiah 14:13ff.

The plight of a true prophet -- Jeremiah 15:10ff.
    Plus a word of HOPE

Obediance to the Sabbath and faithfulness in TEMPLE WORSHIP
    The prerequisites of God's blessing -- Jeremiah 17:19ff.
    Compare Jeremiah 17:9 with Genesis 8:21

"Thou art the Potter -- I am the clay" -- Jeremiah 18:6
    Compare Romans 9:19ff.

An exasperated prophet -- Jeremiah 18:18ff.
    What are the causes of exasperation in the ministry today? Discuss

November 6 - As the Potter molds the clay   Jeremiah 18:1-23; 19:1-13

       7 - A Prophet in stocks -   Jeremiah 19:14-15; 20:1-18
           and mocked -- (604 B.C.)   II Kings 24:1; Jeremiah 47:1-7

       8 - The proud shall be humbled   Jeremiah 48:1-47

       9 - Continuing judgmemt   Jeremiah 49:1-22

      10 - Famous cities --   Jeremiah 49:23-39; II Kings 24:2-6
           deserted in fear (598 B.C.) II Chronicles 36:6-8; Jeremiah 52:28

      11 - Evil extended --   II Kings 24:8-16; Jeremiah 22:24-30
           The end is come   II Chronicles 36:9-10; Esther 2:6

      12 - Captivity becomes a certainty   II Kings 24:17-20; II Chron.36:11-16
                                   Jeremiah 37:1-2; 52:1-2; 21:1-14

****

REFLECTIONS ON READINGS

November 6 through November 12

Internal conflict -- Prophet vs. Priest -- Jeremiah 20
    Compare Jeremiah 20:14 with Job 3:10ff.

Judgments of God against non-Jews and nations -- Jeremiah 47-49
      The faithful are called to suffer with the unfaithful -- Jeremiah 49:12
      Discuss the fairness and/or injustice of that kind of situation
      why do you think God lets that happen? -- Jeremiah 15:15
      Compare Luke 18:1-8 and discuss its meaning

God lets the righteous suffer because of His patience with the unrighteous--
    That's incredible and incomprehensible --
    But THAT'S THE MIND OF GOD

The last King of Judah -- The Southern Kingdom
      Zedekiah -- Rules for 11 years -- II Kings 24:18
      Foolishly defiles the Temple -- Jeremiah 49:34; II Chronicles 36:14
      Would not listen to the Lord's Word and counsel -- II Chronicles 36:11
          Compare Esther 2:6 and Jeremiah 21:1-4

****

November 13 - A final Word to the King   Jeremiah 22:1-23

      14 - A final Word   Jeremiah 23:1-40
          to faithless Shepherds

November 15 - Ruination to Restoration   Jeremiah 24:1-10; 27:12-22

       16 - Don't trust liars   Jeremiah 29:1-32

       17 - Tribulation and captivity   Jeremiah 30:1-24

       18 - There is gladness   Jeremiah 31:1-40
            in the midst of sadness

       19 - The end of the yoke   Jeremiah 28:1-17; 51:59

****

<u>REFLECTIONS ON READINGS</u>

November 13 through November 19

God's awesome challenge for care and concern to the oppressed -- Jeremiah 22;3ff.

The ruined and the REMNANT -- Jeremiah 23:2-6

God's people live in peace! -- Discuss the paradox of "Peace - but no peace".
    Compare Luke 12:49 and John 16:33

The awesome burden of the true prophet -- Jeremiah 23:9ff

A picture of ruination and restoration -- Jeremiah 24; 27:12ff.

Making the best of a bad situation -- Jeremiah 29:4ff.
    "When life serves you lemons - Make lemonade"

70 years of exile -- followed by fulfillment of promise -- Jeremiah 29:10ff.

Mixed emotions -- sadness and gladness because of judgment and restoration
    What does Jeremiah 30 and 31 have to say about our own "Babylon" and
    the promise of heaven

THE MOST PROFOUND TEXT IN ALL OF SCRIPTURE -- Jeremiah 31:34
    Compare Hebrews 8:12 --
    The picture of the High Priestly Jesus in His greatest priestly function

Yoked and unyoked Jeremiah 28 -- compare Matthew 11:28

How and when have you felt "unyoked"? Discuss the feeling

****

<u>BIBLE READING GUIDE</u>
    <u>for BIBLE READING PEOPLE</u>

November 20 - A new and serious prophet   Ezekiel 1:1-28
           appears on the scene

       21 - FULL OF THE SPIRIT   Ezekiel 2:1-10; 3:1-21

November 22 - The glory of God in a vision   Ezekiel 3:22-27; 4:1-7

        23 - Famine, pestilence and sword   Ezekiel 5:1-17; 6:1-7
             Triple threat
             War -- starvation -- disease

        24 - The REMNANT remains   Ezekiel 6:8-14; 7:1-27
             through desolation

        25 - Visions of desperation   Ezekiel 8:1-18; 9:1-11

        26 - The Lord leaves the Temple   Ezekiel 10:1-22

****

REFLECTIONS ON READINGS

November 20 through November 26

EZEKIEL -- a man of profound visions
(591 B.C.) Is there a difference between seeing visions and being a visionary?
        Name and discuss some people whom you think are visionaries today.

To SEE God -- to HEAR the Lord -- and to feel His power --   Ezekiel 1:1-3
        Compare Revelation 4:6
        Compare the four living creatures of Ezekiel 1:5ff with Revelation 5:6ff.

"Mortal Man" --"Don't be afraid"
        The phrase, Ben Adam, is used 80 times in Ezekiel
        Meaning -- "From dust thou art, to dust thou shalt return"

A good word from the prophet --"Do what I tell you!" -- Ezekiel 2 and 3
The awesome task of a spiritual watchman -- Ezekiel 3:16-21

The impressive perspective of the "Installation Service"
        For a corollary study read I Timothy -- especially 3:4ff; 4:1-8

The guilt of Jerusalem on one man -- NOT FAIR -- Ezekiel 4:4-5
        Consider -- the whole world's sin on Jesus -- Romans 5:15

Discuss the TRIPLE THREAT:
        1 - Sickness and hunger
        2 - Punishment by the sword
        3 - Dispersion

Remember the REMNANT -- "I will let some escape" -- Ezekiel 6:8
        The mark or seal of God's protection -- Ezekiel 9:4-6
        Compare Genesis 4:15; Revelation 7:3; 9:4
        An awesome scene -- Ezekiel 10:18ff

If you were to attempt an application of Ezekiel's words in a contemporary sense --
        To whom would these words be basically addressed?

        WHAT A CHALLENGE TO BE GOD'S PEOPLE IN THE MIDST OF GOD'S WORLD

November 27 - Prophesy, O SON OF MAN   Ezekiel 11,1-25

        28 - I am the Lord, I will speak   Ezekiel 12,1-28

        29 - False prophets bring no peace   Ezekiel 13:1-23

        30 - Idols in the heart   Ezekiel 14:1-23

December 1 - You shall know that   Ezekiel 15:1-8
             I AM THE LORD

        2 - A parable -   Ezekiel 16:1-63
            Spiritual Adultery

        3 - A parable in a riddle   Ezekiel 17:1-24

****

REFLECTIONS ON READINGS

November 27 through December 3

The threat -- Ezekiel 11:1-13
        And the promise -- Ezekiel 11:14-21

Compare Ezekiel 12:2 with Matthew 11:14-15; Matthew 13:9; 37-43
        Mark 4:9-12; & vs. 23; Luke 8:8-10; 14:35

The REMNANT -- Ezekiel 12:16; 14:22 -- and the awesome judgment -- Ezekiel 12:28

Don't trust in illusions -- Listen to the Word of the Lord -- Ezekiel 13

A call to LOYALTY -- Ezekiel 14:5; Discuss the ways the Lord calls us to loyalty

"They are to be my people -- I will be their God" -- Ezekiel 14:11
        Compare Revelation 18:4; Romans 9:25; II Corinthians 6:16

The imagery of the vine -- Ezekiel 15 -- Compare John 15:1-8

God's care for His people expressed in the image of marriage -- Ezekiel 16:1-14
        The adulterous response of the people -- Ezekiel 14:15ff.
        Compare Ezekiel 16:48-63 with Matthew 11:20ff and Luke 10:13ff.

A beautiful picture of the Kingdom -- Ezekiel 17:22-24
        Pictures in parables -- Recall the many parables of Jesus -- 30 of them!
        Most predominant -- THE SOWER AND THE SEED -- Matthew 13;18-23; 36-43

Discuss -- What is a parable?

        A parable is a story of very earthly natural happenings --
                Told in such a way as to express a spiritual truth.

December 4 - WORDS of serious judgment   Ezekiel 18:1-32

        5 - Crying for rulers   Ezekiel 19:1-14
            who never ruled

        6 - Mercy from God   Ezekiel 20:1-49
            in spite of rebellion

        7 - Prophesy by word and sword   Ezekiel 21:1-32

        8 - God's indignation revealed   Ezekiel 22:1-31
            in the fire of His wrath

        9 - Debauchery and desolation   Ezekiel 23:1-49

       10 - Fury like a fiery cauldron   Ezekiel 24:1-27

****

REFLECTIONS ON READINGS

December 4 through December 10

WHO IS RESPONSIBLE FOR SIN?? -- Ezekiel 18:1-32
        An articulate description of three generations

A Song of Sorrow -- Ezekiel 19

God keeps His promises! -- Are we as faithful in keeping ours?
        Reflections on the exile -- Ezekiel 20
        Reflections on LAW (Ezekiel 20:36) and GOSPEL (Ezekiel 20:44)

On the Word and the Sword -- Compare Ezekiel 21 with Hebrew 4:12

No whitewashing of sin allowed -- Ezekiel 22:28

The story of two sisters -- Ezekiel 23

The siege of Jerusalem like a boiling cauldrpm -- Ezekiel 24

"THEY WILL KNOW THAT I AM THE LORD" -- Ezekiel 24:27

****

BIBLE READING GUIDE
    for BIBLE READING PEOPLE

December 11 - The final capture (587 B.C.)   Jeremiah 52:3-5 & 29; 32:1-5; 39:1
             and deportation   II Kings 25:1-2; Ezekiel 24:15-18

        12 - Destruction is in the wind   Jeremiah 34:8-22

December 13 - Hooked in the jaw   Ezekiel 29:1-16

       14 - The spoil of riches   Ezekiel 26:1-21

       15 - Merchants & Mariners make merry   Ezekiel 27:1-36

       16 - Pharaoh and Egypt (587 B.C.)   Ezekiel 28:1-19; 30:1-26; 31:1-18
            are going to get it!

       17 - Betrayed, deceived   Jeremiah 37:3-21
            and imprisoned

****

REFLECTIONS ON READINGS

December 11 through December 17

TIME: (587 B.C.) The final capture and deportation to Babylon
       Banished from God's sight -- ?? Doesn't God see everything? Jeremiah 15:3
       Back to the subject of slavery --
            Compare our type of slavery (1863 A.D. with 587 B.C.)

God's drastic action toward the King of Egypt -- Ezekiel 29:1-16; 26:1-21; 27:1ff

Power and riches (commercialism of Tyre) -- no match for the power of God

The prophet Jeremiah betrayed and imprisoned -- Jeremiah 37:11ff.

****

BIBLE READING GUIDE
     for BIBLE READING PEOPLE

December 18 - Interceding for a   Jeremiah 32:6-25
              faithless people

       19 - God's answer -- disappointing   Jeremiah 32;26-44

       20 - God's prophecy of restoration   Jeremiah 33:1-26

       21 - GOOD NEW/BAD NEWS --   Jeremiah 34:1-7; 38:1-27
            for a prophet of God

       22 - The fall; the famine; the flight   Jeremiah 38:28; 39:2-5; 15-18
            (586 B.C.)   II Kings 25:3-5; II Chronicles 36:17

       23 - Persecution of people   Jeremiah 39:6-8; 52:10-14
            and plundering of property   Ezekiel 12:13-14; II Kings 25:6-10

       24 - The Christmas King   Luke 2:8-15;
            and earthly kings   II Kings 25:11-12;II Chron.36:20-21
                                                     Jeremiah 39:9-10; 52:15-16;
                                                     Psalm 94

REFLECTIONS ON READINGS

December 18 through December 24

Do we take God into decision making processes as Jeremiah did? - Jer.32:6-44

A single purpose for life -- Jeremiah 32:38 -- Analyze your purpose of living

The promise of RETURN FOR THE REMNANT -- A word of real Gospel --Jeremiah 32:37ff.

A prophecy of MESSIAH -- Jeremiah 33:14
     Compare Jeremiah 33:22 with Genesis 12:1-3; Genesis 13:14-17

When you are at the bottom of the well, you've got no where to go but UP!
     Jeremiah 38:1-14

The Fall -- the famine and the flight - 586 B.C.- (400 years after Solomon's reign)
     II Kings 25:3-5; Jeremiah 52:6-9; Jeremiah 39:2-10

The poor people left behind -- Jeremiah 52:16; II Kings 25:11

A summary of the whole action -- Psalm 94

****

BIBLE READING GUIDE
for BIBLE READING PEOPLE

December 25 -	Wise men and the KING	Matthew 2:1-12
	Temple treasures taken	II Kings 25:13-17; Jeremiah 52:17-23
	to Babylon	II Chronicles 36:18
26 -	Sad feelings of despair and desolation	Psalm 74
27 -	Heathens harass God's People	Psalm 79; II Kings 25:19-21 Jeremiah 52:24-26
28 -	The sighings of sad, sad, heavy hearted people	Lamentations 1:1-22
29 -	The terrible punishment of an angry God	Lamentations 2:1-22
30 -	Plead for mercy -- not justice	Lamemtations 3:1-66
31 -	Punishment will come to an end	Lamentations 4:1-21; 5:1-22

REJOICE

CONTEMPLATE THE CHRISTMAS STORY -- Luke 2:1-20

Who are the Wise Men of today? -- Matthew 2:1-12

December 25 through December 31

The temple treasures are looted and carted to Babylon
    "To the victor belong the spoils" -- Jeremiah 52:17-26; II Kings 25:13-17
                                      II Chronicles 36:18

Psalms of desolation and despair -- 74 and 79

THE BOOK OF LAMENTATIONS: -- Time of natural disaster -- 586 B.C.
      Chapter 1 - Sighings of a sad, sad people
            2 - God's anger is devastating
                God rejects His altar and deserts the people -- vs.7
            3 - Only God's mercy can help --
                If God exercises justice even God's people are doomed
            4 - In the face of disaster -- pray for mercy
            5 - THROUGH ALL THE YEARS, THE LORD REMAINS --
                A fitting expression for the CLOSE OF THE YEAR

****

HAPPY NEW YEAR

May the Holy Spirit of God bless you in this third year of the

BIBLE READING GUIDE
    for BIBLE READING PEOPLE

January 1 - THE CAPTIVITY -- 586-516 B.C.	II Kings 25:22-24; Jeremiah 39:11-14; 40:1-5
2 - A prophet to the poor	II Kings 25:25; Jeremiah 40:6-16; 41:1-9
3 - Frustrations in captivity	II Kings 25:26; Jeremiah 41:10-18; 42:1-22
4 - The Prophet of God -- ridiculed for lying	Jeremiah 43:1-13
5 - A prophesy of Egypt	Jeremiah 46:13-26
6 - The Jews in Egypt again	Jeremiah 44:1-30
7 - Jerusalem falls -- 586 B.C.	Ezekiel 33:21-33; 25:1-11

****

REFLECTIONS ON READINGS

January 1 through January 7

THE CAPTIVITY: -- A time without a temple -- 586 - 516 B.C.

A paradoxical phenomenon -- JEREMIAH, (God's Man) freed by the conquering enemy,
                              Babylon -- Jeremiah 40:1-6

A revolt and another exile -- to Egypt again, -- Jeremiah 40:13ff; II Kings 25:22ff

When everything else fails -- START PRAYING! -- Jeremiah 42

Nebuchadnezzar, an invading king, shows mercy to Jeremiah, WHY? -- Jeremiah 42:11

No future in Egypt -- Jeremiah 42:19-22
     The prophet captive again -- in Egypt -- Jeremiah 43

EGYPT IS DOOMED -- Jeremiah 46
     Remember the promises to the REMNANT? Jeremiah 46:27ff
     A few of the refugees will return! -- Jeremiah 46:14 & 28

Reliance on the sword is no promise of victory -- Ezekiel 33:26

Enemies of God's people fare no better than the rebellious people of God
     Ezekiel 25 & 28

****

BIBLE READING GUIDE
     for BIBLE READING PEOPLE

January 8 - Prophecies of disaster   Ezekiel 25:12-17; 28:20-26

        9 - The pomp of Egypt -- cast down   Ezekiel 32:1-32

       10 - A fiery furnace   Jeremiah 52:30; Daniel 3:1-30
            and the faith of the fearless

       11 - A peace proclamation   Daniel 4:1-3;Ezekiel 33:1-20;34:1-10

       12 - The promise of restoration   Ezekiel 34:11-31
            for the Kingdom of David

       13 - Mt. Seir (Edom) will fall   Ezekiel 35:1-15; 36:1-15

       14 - Past sins come back to haunt   Ezekiel 36:16-38

****

REFLECTIONS ON READINGS

January 8 through January 14

A Word of Hope in a very despairing, hopeless time-- Ezekiel 28:24-26

Egypt gets her "come-uppance" -- Ezekiel 32
     From power to disgrace -- Ezekiel 32:30

Living the COURAGE OF YOUR CONVICTIONS is done at high risk -- Daniel 3:1-30
        Ready to die for the cause -- Daniel 3:17
        How does the Lord show protection of His saints today?
                Have YOU been personally spared from disaster at any particular time?
                Share the circumstances with those in fellowship around you
        How much risk do we take to show the courage of our convictions?
        Do the results always turn out as well as for the men in the fiery furnace?

A King is converted -- He witnesses to his countrymen -- Daniel 4:1-3
        In our country is it safe for a public official to give testimony to his faith?

Lost sheep because of lousy shepherds -- Ezekiel 34:1-10
        Compare Ezekiel 34:11-16 with John 10:1-16; I Peter2:24-25
                Ezekiel 34:17ff with Matthew 25:32
                Exekiel 34:31 with John 10:16; and Revelation 7:17

You are going to come home soon -- Ezekiel 36:8
        Saved in spite of ourselves -- Ezekiel 36:22
                Review the meaning of the Third Article -- Luther's Small Catechism
        Clean from all sin -- Ezekiel 36:33; compare I John 1:7

****

BIBLE READING GUIDE
        for BIBLE READING PEOPLE

January 15 - The vision of the DRY BONES   Ezekiel 37:1-28

        16 - Gog and Magog turned back   Ezekiel 38:1-21

        17 - Fire and judgment   Ezekiel 39:1-29

        18 - Great visions of a future land   Ezekiel 40:1-41

        19 - Singers and priests --   Ezekiel 40:44-49; 41:1-26
             A restored temple

        20 - The chambers of the Holy Place   Ezekiel 42:1-20; 43:1

        21 - The purpose of a temple   Ezekiel 43:2-27

****

REFLECTIONS ON READINGS

Janauary 15 through January 21

The "Valley of Dry Bones" -- Ezekiel 37
        Obtain, if possible, a record or tape of the spiritual "Dry Bones" as done by
                Fred Waring and his orchestra and chorus. Listen to it in class-Discuss
        RESURRECTION TIME -- Compare I Corinthians 15:42ff and John 5:25 & 28

ARE YOU READY FOR THE RESURRECTION OF ALL FLESH?

The wind and the breath of God
        Compare Genesis 2:7 with Ezekiel 37:7-9
        Does this have any bearing on the answers to the questions:
                "When does a body become a body with a soul?
                "When does a body really die?"

Compare varying concepts of "Temple"
        Ezekiel 37:26; Ephesians 2:19ff; Revelation 21:5

The reunion of Judah (Southern Kingdom) and Israel (Northern Kingdom) Ezekiel 37:15ff
        Defenseless people defended by God -- Ezekiel 38 and 39
                The promise of the return -- Ezekiel 39:25ff.
        The glory of the TEMPLE RESTORED - (The Vision) - Ezekiel-Chapters 40,41,42,43
                Discuss some of the concepts of that vision
                Size and seviceabilityk of the structure
                Sacrificing the animals -- Ezekiel 40;42
                Rooms for the priests ---- Ezekiel 40:45
                The holy place and the altar -- Ezekiel 41:4
                The carvings and the decorations --
                and the wooden altar -- Ezekiel 41:22
                The priests and the sacrifices -- Ezekiel 42:13ff.
                The purpose of the temple -- Ezekiel 43:5ff; Compare Micah 6:6ff.

        THE PERFECT SACRIFICE WITHOUT BLEMISH OR DEFECT -- See Hebrews 4:15ff.

****

BIBLE READING GUIDE
        for BIBLE READING PEOPLE

January 22 - How the priest behave   Ezekiel 44:1-31

        23 - Feasts and offerings   Ezekiel 45:1-25

        24 - The Prince and the People   Ezekiel 46:1-18
             praise God

        25 - The rivers of refreshment   Ezekiel 46:19-24; 47:1-12

        26 - The borders   Ezekiel 47:13-23; 48:1-20
             of the restored lands

        27 - Prophecy upon prophecy   Ezekiel 48:21-35; 29:17-24

        28 - Ethiopia gets its WORD   Ezekiel 30:1-19

****

REFLECTIONS ON READINGS

January 22 through January 28

Details of the priest's service -- Ezekiel 44:10
        What about pastors' property today (Owning parsonage) Ezekiel 44:28; 45:5
                Is there a better way?

Compare Ezekiel 44:1-9 with Revelation 21:22-27

HONESTY -- The basic principle among civil rulers -- Ezekiel 45:10
          How do you think our politicians stack up?

FESTIVAL CELEBRATIONS -- Ezekiel 45:18ff.
          Compare Ezekiel 45:25 with Hebrews 10:11ff.
          Note the phrase -- "Lamb without blemish", Ezekiel 46:13
          Compare this phrase with John 1:29; Hebrews 10:8ff
          Compare the river figure of Ezekiel 47:1-12 with Revelation 22:1-2

JERUSALEM -- "The Lord is here" -- Ezekiel 48:35
          Compare "New Jerusalem" - Revelation 21:2-3 - "Now God's home is with Mankind"
          Compare the "Day of Terror" -- Ezekiel 30:1
               with the "Awful Horror" of Matthew 24:15ff.

****

BIBLE READING GUIDE
     for BIBLE READING PEOPLE

January 29 - Second dream of Nebuchadnezzar   Daniel 4:4-27

       30 - Seven years of madness   II Kings 25:27-30; Daniel 4:28-37
                                                      Jeremiah 52:31-34

February 1 - A time for weeping   Psalm 67; 123; 130; 137
             and a time for prayer

        2 - Dreams in the night   Daniel 8:1-27

        3 - Lost sheep   Isaiah 13:17-22
                                                      Jeremiah 25:12-14; & Chapter 50

        4 - Declaring Zion   Jeremiah 51:1-32
            the work of the Lord

****

REFLECTIONS ON READINGS

January 29 through February 4

Back to dreams and such --
     A frightening dream upsets the comfort and tranquility of prosperity-Dan.4:4ff.
     Daniel's second dream -- Daniel 8
     Daniel's reaction -- Daniel 8:27
     Compare Daniel 4:22 with II Samuel 12:5

Assess the difficulties that accompany accusation and judgment of our personal lives
     What was David's personal response? -- II Samuel 12:13
     What was Nebuchadnezzar's response? - Daniel 4:28; 4:37
     Is there anything akin to this in contemporary experences of civil rulers?

-122-

King Jehoiachin, in exile, is restored to privilege in Babylon
        II Kings 25:27; Jeremiah 52:31-34

The kingdom of Daniel's dream -- Daniel 7ff.
        Babylonia, the Medes, the Persians, Assyria, Syria, Greece and Rome
        Very perplexing -- See Isaiah 13:17

Additional symbolic literary types -- Revelation 13
        "Details of such figures are not to be pressed"
        Book of Daniel, Interpreter's Bible, VI, page 240

Additional PSALMS for reflection especially for this period of time
        Psalm 67 --- Praise and Thanksgiving
                123 -- Need for God's mercy
                130 -- A prayer for a time of despair -- HELP!
                137 -- How can you sing when you're down in the dumps? (Imprecation)

        Compare Isaiah 13:22 with Revelation 18
                Are the Babylons spoken of the same Babylon?
                See also Jeremiah 25:12-14; and Jeremiah 50
                The remnant (refugees) return -- Jeremiah 50:28
                Babylon must fall -- Jeremiah 50 & 51

****

BIBLE READING GUIDE
        for BIBLE READING PEOPLE

February   5 - Judgment on Babylon   Jeremiah 51:33-64

           6 - Handwriting on the wall   Daniel 5:1-16

           7 - Weighed -- and found wanting   Daniel 5:17-31

           8 - PERSIA -- THE WORLD POWER   Isaiah 44:28; Daniel 9:1-19
               (539 - 333 B.C.)
               70 years of desolation for Israel
               (586 - 516 B.C.)

           9 - Praying and confessing   Daniel 9:20-27; Psalm 102

          10 - Time to rebuild   Ezra 1:1-4; 5:13; Psalm 126 & 85
                                                 II Chronicles 36:22-23

          11 - A RETURN TO GLORY   Ezra 1:5-11; 5:14-16; 6:3-5

****

REFLECTIONS ON READINGS

February 5 through February 11

The awesome judgment on Babylon
        God repays evil -- Jeremiah 51:31-54
        Assurance to Jerusalem -- Jeremiah 51:36ff.

Can YOU read the handwriting on the wall? -- Daniel 5
    How do you think the nations of the world today measure up to Daniel 25:25-28?
    The U.S.A.? -- The Church? -- Our congregations?
    How do we measure up in our personal lives?

A new king in Babylon -- Cyrus -- Jeremiah 44:28
    Daniel makes confession for his people -- Daniel 9:3-27
    How do we confess our national sins? -- Our corporate sins?
    with this perspective in mind discuss the "Confessional" in preparation
        for Holy Communion -- Lutheran Book of Worship, Pg.77 & 194

Read Psalm 102 as a confession

The beginning of the turn of events
    A new prophet -- EZRA
    The restoration of life and worship in Jerusalem
        II Chronicles 36:22-23; Ezra 1:1-14; 5:13

Psalms of joy to share because of the Lord's blessing -- 126 & 85

Back to the good old days -- Ezra 1:5-11; 5:14-16; 6:3-5

Review the "ups" and "downs" as you remember them in the history of the church today

****

BIBLE READING GUIDE
    for BIBLE READING PEOPLE

February 12 - Looking into the mouth of a lion   Daniel 6:1-28

        13 - Down by the riverside   Daniel 10:1-21

        14 - The future kingdom in a vision   Daniel 11:1-45

        15 - Turning back to righteousness   Daniel 12:1-13

        16 - The REMNANT returns (536 B.C.)   Ezra 2:1-70

        17 - A whole congregation returns   Nehemiah 7:5-72

        18 - The priests prepare   Nehemiah 12:1-26

****

REFLECTIONS ON READINGS

February 12 through February 18

The patterns of false pretenses -- Daniel 6:11-10
    So -- what's new for us in today's society?
    "Nothing new under the sun" -- Ecclesiastes 1:10

Share some experiences in which you (we) have been delivered from
    "the mouth of the lion".

The essential message from the Word of God --
"God loves you" -- Daniel 10:11;   "Don't be afraid" -- Daniel 10:12; 10:18
Compare Daniel 10:15 with Isaiah 6:5-7
Compare Daniel 10:4-7 with Revelation 19:1 and 11ff.

Discuss Daniel 11 in the light of contemporary circumstances in the Mid-East
What contemporary meaning does Daniel 12 have for us? Compare Matthew 25:31ff
Consider the following types of people
1 - People who make things happen --
2 - People who watch things happen -
3 - People who wonder what happened! (Daneiel 12:4)

The returning REMNANT -- Ezra 2; Nehemiah 7
Discuss the remnant in the light of Daniel 12:1-2; and Revelation 21:22

Preparing for WORSHIP -- The first priority on the return from exile
Ezra 2; Nehemiah 7 and 12
Compare Genesis 8:20; also Genesis 12:7-8; 13:4

****

BIBLE READING GUIDE
for BIBLE READING PEOPLE

February 19 - The Altar rebuilt   Ezra 3:1-13; Psalm 87

       20 - The beauty of the Tabernacle   Psalm 84; 107

       21 - Rebuilding interrupted   Psalm 66:1-20; 125; Ezra 4:1-5

       22 - Temple building delayed   Ezra 4:6-24

       23 - A prophet stirs the people   Psalm 129:1-8; Ezra 5:1-2
                                               Haggai 1:1-15

       24 - Rebuilding resumes (521 B.C.)   Haggai 2:1-23; Zechariah 1:1-6

       25 - Completion in sight   Zechariah 1:7-21; 4:6-10

****

REFLECTIONS ON READINGS

February 19 through February 25

Daily sacrifices renewed on the rebuilt Altar of God -- Ezra 3:1-13
Sacrifices included the giving of money -- Ezra 3:7
The people were so happy they cried -- Ezra 3:12-13
Are there times when you shared that feeling? Disuss the circumstances

The joy of Jerusalem (Gentiles included) -- Psalm 87
Compare Revelation 21:2 and 24
Love for worship in the temple of God -- Psalm 84
Good reasons for thanksgiving -- Psalm 66 and 107

Discuss the problem "We worship the same God you worship" -- Ezra 4:1-5
    The emotions -- the animosity -- does it happen in contemporary settings?

Taxation and troublemakers -- Ezra 4:6-24
    Opposition to rebuilding the city and the Temple

Entrance of two new prophets -- (contemporaries of Ezra)
    HAGGAI -- 520 B.C. -- "Rebuild the Temple"
        The Temple the center of the whole system -- Haggai 1:1-15
    Zerubbabel -- The civil ruler and king
    ZECHARIAH --- 1:1-6

****

BIBLE READING GUIDE
    for BIBLE READING PEOPLE

February 26 - A picture of the atoning Christ   Zechariah 2:1-13; 3:1-10

        27 - Olive trees and candlesticks   Zechariah 4:1-14; 5:1-11

        28 - Chariots and crowns   Zechariah 6:1-13

March   1 - Renewing the decree - 519 B.C.   Ezra 5:3-17; 6:6-18

         2 - They would not hear - How sad!   Zechariah 7:1-14

         3 - The Lord gets furious --   Zechariah 8:1-23;
             And jealous

****

REFLECTIONS ON READINGS

February 26 through March 3

GOD'S LOVE FOR JERUSALEM -- Zechariah 1:7-11

Zerubbabel -- Leader of the exiled people -- Zechariah 4:6-10
    Compare Ephesians 2:16ff
    God's special protection for his people -- Zechariah 2:1-13
    Compare Zechariah 2:10 with Revelation 21:3

SATAN versus the SAVIOR -- Zechariah 3:1-2
    Compare Romans 8:31ff
    Compare Zechariah 3:3ff with II Corinthians 5:21
        Zechariah 4:1-14 with Revelation 1:12; 2:1

The visions of scrolls and a basketful of wickedness -- Zechariah 5:1-11

The Branch and the Temple -- Zechariah 6:12
    Compare the measuring of Zechariah 2:1 with Revelation 11:1-4
        The witnesses of Zechariah 4:14 with Revelation 11:4ff

-126-

Orders to build substantiated in the record of Cyrus -- Ezra 5 and 6
        Rededication of the Temple -- Ezra 6:16
        Compare with the first dedication -- I Kings 8:62ff; II Chronicles 7:4ff.

Religious insincerity the root of the problem --
        Refusal to listen -- Zechariah 7:11ff.

The paradox of God's anger and God's love -- Zechariah 8:1-23
        Discuss: Can God really "hate" (Psalm 5:5) and "love" (I John 4:7ff)
            at the same time?

****

BIBLE READING GUIDE
        for BIBLE READING PEOPLE

March   4 - THE TEMPLE IS DEDICATED -- 516 B.C. Ezra 6:19-22; Psalm 146:11
            WITH GREAT JOY   RESTORATION PERIOD (516 - 400 B.C)

        5 - Praise God -- PRAISE GOD   Psalm 112; 113; 116;   117:1-2
            PRAISE GOD

        6 - The KING OF KINGS   Zechariah 9:1-17
            against the kings (494 B.C.)

        7 - The good shepherd is turned away   Zechariah 1:1-12; 11:1-17

        8 - Once again God delivers Israel   Zechariah 12:1-14; 13:1-9

        9 - Again the people praise God   Zechariah 14:1-21

       10 - A Queen rebells (485 B.C.)   Esther 1:1-22

****

REFLECTIONS ON READINGS

March 4   through March 10

The Temple is ready -- Let's Celebrate -- Ezra 6:19-22
        The Passover is remembered and reinstituted once again
        How graciously the Lord invites us inspite of our lapses and failures!

When the temple is ready -- GOD'S PEOPLE SING AND REJOICE
        Why so much singing in the worship of our God?
        Study Psalm 146 -- the full scope of God's Service to humankind
        Compare Luke 4:16-20; and Isaiah 61:3
        Psalm 111 -- Heartfelt thanks in the presence of God's people
                112 -- The blessing of a righteous person
                113 -- GOD IS GOD -- PRAISE HIM!
                116 -- Saved from death? -- Praise God in the midst of other people
                        We call it the "communion of saints"
                117 -- Praise Him -- ALL PEOPLE -- ALL NATIONS

Rejoicing in restoration -- Zechariah 9:1-13
        Compare Matthew 21:1-11; Mark 11:1-11; John 12:12-19

No longer does the church fight its battles at the point of a sword - Zechariah 9:10

The mysterious picture of the shepherd -- Zechariah 11:4ff; 13; Compare John 10

The greatest blessing -- a spirit of mercy and prayer -- Zechariah 12:10

Analyze the possibilities -- Zechariah 14
        Is it historical? -- Messianic? Or Apocalyptic?

THE BOOK OF ESTHER -- Time of Xerxes (Ahasuerus) -- 485 - 465 B.C.
        Historical problems -- Many theories
                Should the Book of Esther be placed earlier in the chronicles of Jewish
                history? Jewish history places Esther as a contemporary of Daniel
        Compare Vashti, Esther, and Abigail of I Samuel 25
                Queen Vashti -- The world's first feminist? -- Esther 1
                Compare New Testament Ephesians 5:21-33

****

BIBLE READING GUIDE
    for BIBLE READING PEOPLE

March 11 - Searching for a new queen   Esther 2:1-11

        12 - Esther wins the queen's crown   Esther 2:12-23

        13 - Conspiracy in the King's court   Esther 3: 1-15
             (474 B.C.)

        14 - The Jews oppressed --   Esther 4:1-17
             mourning and fasting

        15 - Intercession by the Jewish   Esther 5:1-14
             Queen in the Gentile Court

        16 - A sleepless night   Esther 6:1-14

        17 - Conspiracy taken captive --   Esther 7:1-10; 8:1-14
             Freedom exalted!

****

REFLECTIONS ON READINGS

March 11 through March 17

"Take the girl you like the best" -- Esther 2:4
        What advice is the best advice in choosing a girl today?

A beautiful girl (Esther 2:7) -- becomes Queen (Esther 2:17)

Hostility in high places results in a hanging -- Esther 2:21ff

Mordecai akin to Daniel -- dares to be different -- Esther 3:2
        "Kill every Jew" -- forerunner of the "Holocaust"?
        Discuss the tolerance of races and nationalities -- Then and NOW!

The destinies of men and women -- "For a time like this"
        What is the particular purpose for our calling as Christians?
                Consider Colossians 1:16-17
        Fasting and praying among God"s people -- Esther 4:16

A female JEW in a male GENTILE court -- Esther 5:11ff.

Saved by the record -- Esther 6:1ff.
        Conspiracy thwarted -- FREEDOM EXALTED -- Esther 7 & 8
        The feast of Purim -- Esther 3:7; 9:20ff.

****

BIBLE READING GUIDE
        for BIBLE READING PEOPLE

March 18 - Rejoicing and shameful revenge   Esther 8:15-17; 9:1-13

        19 - Celebration and feasting   Esther 9:16-27

        20 - Remember these days   Esther 9:28-32;
             "Those were the days, my friends"

        21 - The prophet leads the praising   Ezra 7:11-28
             (459 B.C.)

        22 - Reunion in prayer   Ezra 8:1-23

        23 - Temple treasures treated with care   Ezra 8:24-31; 7:6-10

        24 - Renewal and reform   Ezra 8:32-36; 9:1-15
             in prayer and confession

****

REFLECTIONS ON READINGS

March 18 through March 24

A power struggle to the "nth" degree -- Esther 9:1ff
        Total capitulation -- Esther 9:12
        Key words -- Power (vs.1); Organize (vs.2) Fear (vs.3)
        Interesting concepts:
                75,800 killed! -- Was it vengeance?
                        or -- Was it righteous indignation?
                No looting! Esther 9 :10 & 15
        Celebrate the victory -- from grief and despair to joy and happiness,
                                peace and security

A generous offer from the government -- Ezra 7
    A prophet praises God for <u>grace</u> and <u>courage</u> among the people -- Ezra 7:27-28

<u>REVIVAL TIME: People to serve God in the temple</u> Ezra 8:17
    A time for <u>fasting and prayer</u> Ezra 8:21ff.
    A time for <u>giving</u> -- Ezra 8:24ff.
    A time for <u>Temple worship</u> -- Ezra 8:33 & 36
        Discuss the importance of "Going to church"

The problem of mixed marriages -- Ezra 9 and 10

A model <u>CONFESSION</u> -- Ezra 9:6ff.

****

<u>BIBLE READING GUIDE</u>
    <u>for BIBLE READING PEOPLE</u>

March 25 - A national gathering of repentance   Ezra 10:1-15

    26 - Priest and strange women   Ezra 10:16-44

    27 - We have sinned against Thee --   Nehemiah 1:1-11
         BE MERCIFUL

    28 - Inspection of the ruins (444 B.C.)   Nehemiah 2:1-20; 5:14

    29 - Construction crews conscripted   Nehemiah 3:1-32

    30 - Ridicule and conspiracy   Nehemiah 4:1-23
         gets in the way

    31 - Greediness and heartlessness   Nehemiah 5:1-19
         in the ranks of God's people

****

<u>REFLECTIONS ON READINGS</u>

March 25 through March 31

Gather the people for repentance -- Ezra 10:7
    Review the "Confession and Absolution" segment of our Lutheran Liturgy
    Does it express what Ezra tried to convey to his people? Discuss

<u>NEHEMIAH</u> -- Prophet of God and Governor of the people -- (465 - 423 B.C.)
    Concern for Jerusalem expressed in confession and prayer for mercy - Neh.1:1-11
    "I prayed" -- "Then I said" -- Nehemiah 2:4-5
    What an excellent model for conversing with God -<u>PRAY</u>-Then state your business!
    What a beautiful feeling -- "God was with me" -- Nehemiah 2:8
    Discuss the ways in which you have felt the presence of God in your life

A personal inspection -- Nehemiah 2:11
    Inspired by God (Nehemiah 2:12) -- "Let's start rebuilding" Nehemiah 2:18

Building takes team work and cooperation -- Nehemiah 3
        Opposition met with prayer and a song -- Nehemiah 4
                How about "A Mighty Fortress" or "We Shall Overcome"?
                "Don't be afraid" -- Nehemiah 4:14
                "God will fight for us" -- Nehemiah 4:20
                Working with weapons in hand -- Nehemiah 4:21-23
        Internal dissension and a heavy mortgage -- Nehemiah 5
                Dealing with the problem -- Nehemiah 5:6-19

****

BIBLE READING GUIDE
        for BIBLE READING PEOPLE

April 1 - This work was of God (444 B.C.)   Nehemiah 6:1-19

      2 - Keeping watch as the exile ends   Nehemiah 7:1-72;I Chronicles 9:2-34

      3 - Jerusalem -- the treasured city   Nehemiah 11:1-36

      4 - THE WORD WAS READ --   Nehemiah 7:73; 8:1-12
          The people listened!

      5 - Publish and proclaim   Nehemiah 8:13-18
          the Word of the Lord

      6 - The goodness of God reviewed   Nehemiah 9:1-38
          with fasting and repenting

      7 - Renewal and recommitment   Nehemiah 10:1-39

****

REFLECTIONS ON READINGS

April 1 through April 7

Trick or treat -- Getting to the truth -- Nehemiah 6:1-9 -- (444 B.C.)

A true test of character -- Nehemiah 6:11-19
        Something to ponder -- the difference between character and reputation

Attention to the Temple in times of distress -- Nehemiah 7:1-4; I Chronicles 9:28ff

THE WORD IN WORSHIP -- Nehemiah 8:18
        True worship -- praise -- confession -- Nehemiah 9:5
        Fulfillment of promise -- compare Genesis 15:5 with Nehemiah 9:23
        God can be trusted! -- Nehemiah 9:32-35
                What would you say of the people?

Put it into writing and sign the agreement -- Nehemiah 9:38; 10
        Summary -- "We will not neglect the House of the Lord" -- Nehemiah 10:39
        Reflect on: How well do we care for the House of the Lord, our church building
                How frequently am I present when the Lord calls to worship?

April 8 - Rededication with gladness   Nehemiah 12:1-43

       9 - Praising God   Psalm 147; 148
           for promises fulfilled

      10 - Preparation for worship   Psalm 149; 150
                                                Nehemiah 12:44-47; 13:1-3

      11 - The WORD hidden in the heart   Psalm 119:1-40

      12 - Remember the WORD   Psalm 119:41-88

      13 - The WORD of God is a faithful WORD   Psalm 119:89-136

      14 - The Lord is righteous --   Psalm 119:137-176
           WE CAN REJOICE!   Psalm 1:1-6

****

REFLECTIONS ON READINGS

April 8 through April 14

A REDEDICATION SERVICE of joy and thanksgiving -- Nehemiah 12

        Give attention to the order of service -- Compare it with our own
                Processional to the temple
                Hymns of thanksgiving -- choir response
                Instrumental music -- Cymbals and harps
                Families of singers
                Ritual purification -- Compare with our communion
                Sacrifices offered
                Tithing -- first fruits -- daily gifts
                People filled with joy
                Women and children included
                The joyful noise they made could be heard for miles

LORD--RENEW THAT SPIRIT IN THE PEOPLE OF YOUR CHURCH TODAY!!

A review of the hymns (Psalms) of praise
        Psalm 147 - The people of God can't help but worship
                148 - The universe and all nature gives praise to Him
                149 - Create new songs -- Dance to the glory of God
                150 - "Go to church" with your worship and praise
                119 - Vs.1-40 The WORD in the heart; (41-80) The WORD remembered
                      (81-88) A WORD of despair; (89-136) The WORD can be trusted
                      (136-176) The WORD is a righteous WORD
                      It delivers (145-152) - It helps (153-160) and (169-176)
                                            It calls us to dedication (161-168)
                120 - Help me from liars and deceivers
        Psalm 1:1-- 6: True happiness is in obeying the WORD
                        Condemnation follows without it

A CONTEMPORARY PSALM FOR TODAY'S LIVING
(A paraphrase of Psalm 23)

The Lord is my security.
    He fills all my need.
He is my carpeted floor
    and the foam rubber in my mattress.
He keeps the water running in my
    air conditioner -- and keeps me cool.
He strengthens and forgives me when I feel guilty
    and tells me how to live right
    that in His mercy I may magnify Him!
Even though I know I"m going to die -
    I'm not afraid
    For You are with me -- even in death.
Even when you discipline me
    and direct me -- I feel safe.
When the going gets tough because people
    pick on me -- You give me big meals
You massage my brow when I am worried.
    I have more than I can drink.
How good God is, and I know He is going
    to bless me with His steadfast love
    as long as I live in this old world
And when that's over, I'm going to have the
    biggest and best house yet--
    Because it's God's house and
    I'm going to live in it forever!

                                Leo E. Wehrspann

****

BIBLE READING GUIDE
    for BIBLE READING PEOPLE

April 15 - The Temple and TITHING   Nehemiah 13:4-22

    16 - Watch whom you marry   Nehemiah 13:23-31

    17 - False priests lead to   Malachi 1:1-14; 2:1-9
         pollution -- in worship

    18 - God gets tired of our games   Malachi 2:10-17; 3:1-18

    19 - It's time to talk RESURRECTION   Malachi 4:1-6

    20 - END OF THE OLD TESTAMENT ERA
         Review and think on these things
             - Greece - the world power (333 to 63 B.C.)
             - Rome   - the world power (63 B.C. to 476 A.D.)

REFLECTIONS ON READINGS

April 15 through 20

God turns curses into blessings -- Nehemiah 13:2
        Compare Numbers 24:10; 22-25

Support the musicians and the priesthood -- Nehemiah 13:10
        Theology, supported with music, is the grand march of
                the Holy Christian Church through time and eternity

Choosing a marriage partner is a major decision
        Next to your decision to choose Christ --
                Your choice of a life partner is the most important decision of life
        Consider Solomon -- Nehemiah 13:25ff.
        If in the New Testament, Christians are the New Israel -- How would you
        apply the Old Testament law in a contemporary sense?

MALACHI -- The last of the Old Testament prophets

        The Lord's pledge of His love -- Malachi 1:2
        If God is love -- how could he possibly "hate Esau and his descendants"?
        God deserves our very best -- Malachi 1:6-8
        Pretension is one of mankind's worst sins
        Respect for God follows His blessing -- Malachi 2:2-5
        A marriage is a commitment and promise TO BE FAITHFUL -- Malachi 2:13-16

A preview and prophecy of the future -- Malachi 3:1-5

Failing to tithe is short changing and cheating God -- Malachi 3:8-12
        You cannot out give God! -- Malachi 3:10ff.

        IF WE CAN TRUST THE WORD OF GOD FOR THE SALVATION OF OUR SOULS THROUGH THE
        MESSAGE OF REDEMPTION IN JESUS CHRIST --

        WHY CAN'T WE TRUST THAT SAME WORD OF PROMISE HE GIVES ABOUT OUR GIVING?

Review Chapter 4 once again:

        How do you interpret? -- Literalistic? Messianic? Apocolyptic?

Review your impressions of what you have read in the Old Testament Scripture:

        Have you grown in your confidence of salvation?
        Have you become more aware of personal sins and the sins of God's people?
        Are you frightened by God's persistent judgment?
        Are you more appreciative (and relieved) by the promises of GRACE AND MERCY

Does the review of Old Testament history strengthen or diminish our theological
        view of LAW/GOSPEL interpretion of the Holy Scripture?
        Share your views with those around you. --
        Discuss concepts that still intrigue you from this Old Testement study.

GET READY FOR THE NEW TESTAMENT'S GOOD NEWS

April 21 - The life of our Lord   Matthew 1:1-17; Mark 1:1;
                                            Luke 1:1-4; 3:23-28; John 1:1-5

        22 - Important announcements   Luke 1:5-25

        23 - "YOU WILL NAME HIM JESUS"   Luke 1:46-80

        24 - My soul is glad --   Luke 1:46-80
             I have a Savior

        25 - The birthday of a King   Matthew 1:18-24; Luke 2:1-20

        26 - The Lord receives His own gift   Luke 2:21-38

        27 - Early trouble   Matthew 2:1-23; Luke 2:39-40

        28 - Outsmarting the smartest   Luke 2:41-52

****

REFLECTIONS ON READINGS

April 21 through April 28

An orderly account of THE BEGINNINGS OF THE EARTHLY LIFE OF JESUS -- Luke 1:3
        Matthew 1:1-17; Mark 1:1; Luke 1:1-25; 3:23-38; John 1:1-5

Speechless in the face of the WORD OF THE LORD --   Luke 1:19-20

A NAME THAT IS ABOVE EVERY NAME Luke 2:21; Matthew 1:21; Compare Philippians 2:4ff.

Mary's magnificent music ---   Sing the song of salvation --- Luke 1:46-55

The birthday of the GREATEST KING ever born -- Luke 1:1-20; Matthew 1:18-24
      Fulfillment of Old Testament rites -- Luke 2:22ff.
      THE PURPOSE OF HIS LIFE -- Luke 2:25ff.

Early trouble in the Lord's life -- Matthew 2:1-23

Twelve years go by in a hurry -- Luke 2:39-52

****

April 29 - A renegade for redemption   Matthew 3:1-6; Mark 1:2-6
                                            John 1:19-28; 1:6-18

        30 - The Man, the Message,   MAtthew 3:7-12; Luke 3:7-18;
            and the MISSION   John 1:19-28

May 1 – Baptism followed with the FIRE OF TEMPTATION		Matthew 3:13-17; 4:1-11; Mark 1:9-13; Luke 3:21-34
2 – The first to be called DISCIPLES		Luke 4:1-15; John 1:29-51
3 – The beginning of MIRACLES		John 2:1-25
4 – Conversion and new birth		John 3:1-24
5 – Witnessing pays -- and costs		John 3:25-36; 4:1-25; Luke 3:19-20

****

REFLECTIONS ON READINGS

April 29 through May 5

<u>JOHN THE BAPTIST</u>--The man in the front-line of witnessing-(pointing people to Jesus)
Matthew 3:1-6; Mark 1:2-6; Luke 3:1-6; John 1:16-18

Let's talk about this man of God
How was He received in his time?
How do you think he would be received today?
Of today's preachers and church leaders, who do you think would most
accurately fit the characteristics of John the Baptist?
Check the prophetic pronouncement of Isaiah 40:3-8
Check the number of years separating Isaiah and John

Let's talk about the MESSAGE of this man –Matt.3:7-12;Luke 3:7-18;John 1:19-28
"You snakes" -- Is that the way to win friends and influence people?
How about trust in ancestors?
Discuss water baptism and spirit baptism

THE BAPTISM OF JESUS -- Matthew 3:13-17; Mark 9:1-11
Discuss:-- The need for the baptism of Jesus
Does the baptism of Jesus really prove baptism only by immersion?
Discuss the presence of the Holy Spirit -- At Christ's baptism
At our own baptism

The wilderness and Temptation experience -- Matt.4:1-11; Mark 1:12-13; Luke 4:1-13
In what way does the devil influence (tempt) us in our lives?
In what way does the HOLY SPIRIT influence (direct) our lives?
Refer to Matthew 4:1 and reflect on Ephesians 6:10ff.

Discuss the following concepts on the basis of the week's readings
"Lamb of God" -- "Sins of the world" -- "Son of God"
Is there a difference between a believer and a disciple?
Personal witnessing with friends -- and family
Conversion and new birth -- John 3:1-36
Judgment and salvation
The high cost of witnessing -- Luke 3:18-20
Commercialism in the Church today -- John 2,13ff.
Review the experience of the miracle -- John 2:1-12
Discuss the LAW/GOSPEL content of John 4:1-26

BIBLE READING GUIDE
    for BIBLE READING PEOPLE

May 6 - Jesus concern for the lost   John 4:27-54; Matthew 4:12-17
         and the dying   Mark 1:14-15; Luke 4:14-15

     7 - The preaching of the greatest   Luke 4:16-20
         preacher is rejected

     8 - Time to stop fishing   Matthew 4:18-22; Mark 1:16-22
                                               Luke 5:1-11

     9 - Days of miracles and healing   Matthew 8:14-17; Mark 1:23-34
                                               Luke 4:31-37

    10 - On tour with the Gospel   Matthew 4:23-25; Mark 1:35-39
                                               Luke 4:38-44

    11 - Preaching and healing   Matthew 8:2-4; 9:1-8
                                               Mark 1:40-45; Luke 5:12-16

    12 - Blasphemy? or God's power?   Matthew 9:9-13; Mark 2:1-12
                                               Luke 5:17-26

****

REFLECTIONS ON READINGS

May 6 through May 12

On witnessing and healing -- Share some of your own experiences in witnessing
                             Share some of your experiences of God's healing for you
                             How were you first witnessed to?
                             How did you first come to Christ?
                             When did you first acknowledge Him as Savior?

A good sermon gets positive and negative responses
     Review Luke 4:16-30; Matthew 4:18-22; Mark 1:16-22

        Discuss - How does Jesus "call" today?
                  How does Jesus "heal" today?
                  The fish story of Luke 5:1-11
                  The problems of evil spirits -- then -- and now
                      Matthew 8:14-17; Mark 1:21-34; Luke 4:31-37
                  Compare Isaiah 53:4

How does the Christian Church "take the Gospel on the Road" today? Luke 4:42-44

Physical healing or spiritual forgiveness -- What's most important? Discuss
     Is it possible that they go hand in hand?   Matthew 9:1-8

Who belongs to the CHURCH? -- Matthew 9:9-13
     Why does the church today have difficulty
          relating to the "up and outs" as well as the "down and outs"

May 13 - Questions begin to pour in   Matthew 9:14-17; Mark2:13-22
                                             Luke 5:27-39

     14 - Healing waters   John 5:1-18

     15 - The meaning of life and resurrection   John 5:19-47

     16 - The LAW above the law   Matthew 12:1-14; Mark;2:23-27; 3:1-6
                                             Luke 6:1-12

     17 - The Kingdom grows --   Matthew 12:15-21; Mark 3:7-19
          The first twelve apostles   Luke 6:6-14

     18 - The best known sermon of Jesus   Matthew 5:1-48; Luke 6:17-19

     19 - The lessons of the Lord   Matthew 6:1-34

****

REFLECTIONS ON READINGS

May 13 through May 19

Questions and answers:

     About outcasts -- Matthew 9:9-13; Mark 2:13-17; Luke 5:27-32
     About fasting -- Matthew 9:14-17; Mark 2:18-22; Luke 5:27-32
     About healing -- John 5:1-18
     About Sabbath -- Matthew 12:1-14; Mark 2:23-28; 3:1-6;
                       Luke 6:1-11; John 5:1-18
                       Consider Colossians 2:16-23
     About authority - John 5:19-47
          and resurrection -- Compare John 5:24-29 with Revelation 20:4-6
     About the Kingdom:
          The first disciples -- Mark 3:13-19; Luke 6:12-16
          The servant King ---- Matthew 12:15-21
     About happiness - The Sermon on the Mount -- Matthew 5:1-48; Luke 6:20-34

****

May 20 - Teaching with authority   Matthew 7:1-29

     21 - Parallels of the sermon   Matthew 8:1; Luke 6:20-49

     22 - A soldier is healed   Matthew 8:5-13; Luke 7:1-13

     23 - A preacher in prison   Matthew 11:2-15; Luke 7:18-30

     24 - Condemnation and invitation   Matthew 11:16-30; Luke 7:31-35

25 - Anointing and glad tidings	Matthew 12:22-30; Mark 3:28-35 Luke 7:36-50
26 - Serious sins and silly sign seeking	Matthew 12:31-50; Mark 3:28-35 Luke 8:19-21

****

REFLECTIONS ON READINGS

May 20 through May 26

HE TAUGHT WITH AUTHORITY -- Matthew 7:1-29

    About Judging -- Matthew 7:1-6
            Do we dare point out one another's faults?
            What does this have to say about LAW/GOSPEL interpretation of the WORD?
            About Prayers -- Matt 7:7-12
            "Who is saved"? -- Matthew 7:13-14
            Fruit-bearing ---- Matthew 7:15-18
            Hypocrites ------ Matthew 7:21-23
            Soundness   ------ Matthew 7:24-26

    Discuss the questions that arise from any of these subjects -- e.g. What is
            the most important act of obedience to the Father? -- (See John 6:40ff.)

More on healing -- Matthew 8:1-13; Luke 7:1-17

A PREACHER IN PRISON gets a little discouraged -- Matthew 11:2-19; Luke 7:18-30
        Do you know anyone who has gone to prison for his/her faith?
        How much risk are you willing to take to be a witness for Jesus?

A drastic judgment of God upon whole cities -- Matthew 11:20-24

A BEAUTIFUL GOSPEL INVITATION -- Matthew 11:25-30
        Have you felt the strength of that message of Jesus? How and in what way?

What is the sin against the Holy Spirit? Discuss -- Matthew 12:30ff; Mark 3:28ff

Do we need to have proof? Can you ever prove faith? Matthew 12:38ff.

Discuss the accusation against Jesus, "He's gone mad!" -- Mark 3:20ff.

Wrong company gets you a bad name -- Luke 7:36ff.

A picture of the family of Jesus -- Who is the family of Jesus? Luke 8:19-21

A famous parable -- THE SOWER AND THE SEED -- Matthew 13:1-13;Mark 4:1-25;Luke 8;6ff
        What does this have to say about spiritual growth in the lives of Christians?
        How do you handle the problem of the "drop-out" in your church?
        Consider the faithful -- In what ways do the "bring forth fruit"?
                Consider the ways in which each of us can bring forth "more" fruit

May 27 - Sowers and seeds   Matthew 13:1-23

    28 - Sowers and seeds (Mark's Version)   Mark 4:1-25

    29 - The paraable of seeds and secrets   Luke 8:4-18; Mark 4:26-29

    30 - Three powerful parables   Matthew 13:24-33; Mark 4:30-32

    31 - The purpose of parables   Matthew 13:34-44; Mark 4:33-34

June 1 - Parables and miracles   Matthew 13:45-53; 8:18-27
                                                 Mark 4:35-41; Luke 8:22-25

     2 - Demons and evil spirits   Matthew 8:28-34; Mark 5:1-26

****

REFLECTIONS ON READINGS

May 27 through June 2

Discuss the use of parables in the teachlings of Jesus --
        Sower and Seed -- Matthew 13:18-23; Mark 4:13-20; Luke 8:4-15
        Weeds -- In the Church? Matthew 13:24-33
        Mustard seed -- Mark 4:30-32

WHEN DISCUSSING PARABLES ALWAYS ASK: WHAT ARE THE SPIRITUAL IMPLICATIONS?
                                       WHAT WAS JESUS REALLY TRYING TO SAY?

Study the explanatory system that Jesus used -- Matthew 13:34-44; Mark 4:33-34

More parables to study:
        The pearl -- Matthew 13:45-46
        the net --- Mathew 13:47-53
        Funeral practices -- Matthew 8:18-22

More miracles to study:
        Calming the sea -- Matthew 8:23-27; Mark 4:35-41; Luke 8:22-25
        To get the fullest meaning continue to ask the question:
            "What are the spiritual implication of the lesson?"

****

BIBLE READING GUIDE
    for BIBLE READING PEOPLE

June 3 - Devils depart --   Luke 8:26-39
         by the command of the Lord

     4 - POWER OVER DEATH   Matthew 9:18-26; Mark 5:21-43

     5 - A parallel of power   Matthew 9:27-34; 54-58; Luke 8:40-56

6 - Prophetic preaching ignored	Matthew 9:35-38;10:1-15;Mark 6:1-11
7 - Preach and heal -- and don't be afraid	Matthew 10:16-42; Luke 9:1-6
8 - A powerful witness -- leads to persecution	Matthew 11:1; 14:1-12; Mark 6:12-29; Luke 9:7-9
9 - What a grand picnic -- food left over!	Matthew 14:13-21; Mark 6:30-44 Luke 9:10;17

****

REFLECTIONS ON READINGS

June 3 through June 9

IS THE DEVIL FOR REAL?? -- Matthew 8:28-34; Mark 5:1-20; Luke 8:26-39
  Use a concordance and check the passages that refer to the devil and the
  action he stirs up in the world and the universe
    Do we take the devil seriously in our sacred and secular life?
    How can we defeat the influence of the devil in our lives?
    What are the ways in which the devil distorts the Word of God?

How can we live in the confidence of power over death? --   Discuss -- Mark 5:21-43;
                             Luke 8:40-56

Proper respect for a prophet -- Matthew 13:38-53
  In what ways to we ignore prophetic preaching? -- Mark 6:1-6
  "They rejected him -- They did not have faith"!

Prayer for the people -- Matthew 9:35-38

SPEND A FEW MOMENTS DISCUSSING WITNESSING AND WORKING IN THE KINGDOM
  Witnessing leads to problems -- Share some of your own experiences
  When do we get into trouble witnessing?
  Discuss that in the context of LAW/GOSPEL application
    Matthew 14:1-12; Mark 6:14-29; Luke 9:6-9

A Grand picnic -- a good time had by all -- Lots of food left-over
  Spiritualize the story -- What are the lessons to be learned?
    Matthew 14:13ff; Mark 6:30-44; Luke 9:10-17; John 6:1-15

****

BIBLE READING GUIDE
  for BIBLE READING PEOPLE

June 10 - Prayer time in the mountain	Matthew 14:22-33; Mark 6:45-52 John 6:1-15
11 - Bread for life or Bread for LIFE	Matthew 14:34-36; Mark 6:53-56 John 6:15-44

12 - Believe it and enjoy LIFE -- Deny it and DIE	Matthew 15:1-20; John 6:45-71
13 - Hypocrites and healing	Matthew 15:1-20; Mark 7:1-23
14 - Many - Many - More miracles	Matthew 15:29-38; Mark 7:24-37;8:1-9
15 - Faith does not need SIGNS for proof	Matthew 16:1-12; Mark 8:10-26
16 - A great confession	Matthew 16:13-28; Mark 8:27-33; Luke 9:18-22

****

REFLECTIONS ON READINGS

June 10 through June 16

"DON't BE AFRAID" Discuss that concept as revealed in Matthew 14:27

Who are the ones who "get saved"? Compare Matthew 14:30 with Acts 2:21

Spiritualize the miracle incident of Matthew 24:22-32; Mark 6:45-52

Which is the most important in YOUR life -- BREAD for life? Or BREAD FOR LIFE??
        Discuss that in the light of John 6:22-71 and Matthew 16:5-12

Discuss the healings and miracles as signs or proof of Christ's Divine Nature
        Review the following passages -- Matthew 14:34-36; Mark 6:53-56
                        Compare -- John 6:30 Matthew 16:1-4; Mark 8:11-13

Discuss false teachings as evidence of spiritual sickness -- Matthew 15:1-20;
                                                                Mark 7:1-23
Can all sickness be overcome by faith? Matthew 15:21-38; Mark 7:24-37

GREAT CONFESSIONS OF FAITH -- Matthew 16:13-28; Mark 8:27-33; Luke 9:18-20

****

BIBLE READING GUIDE
    for BIBLE READING PEOPLE

June 17 - UP on a high ----- Mountain A tremendous spiritual retreat	Mattew 17:1-8; Mark 8:34-38; 9:1-8 Luke 9:23-36
18 - Driving out demons	Matthew 17:9-21; Mark 9:9-29
19 - Amazed at the mighty power	Matthew 17:22-27; Mark 9:30-32 Luke 9:37-45
20 - Humility and forgiveness	Matthew 18:1-14; Mark 9:34-50; Luke 9:46-50

June 21 - Forgiveness and prayer   Matthew 18:15-35

  22 - Unbelievers make no marks   John 7:1-53

  23 - Sin and Salvation --   John 8:1-30
       Light and Darkness

****

REFLECTIONS ON READINGS

June 17 through June 23

Have you ever had a mountain top experience? -- With Jesus? Discuss
      Meditate on THE TRANSFIGURATION -- Matthew 17:1-8; Mark 9:1-13; John 9:26-28
            WHAT A GLORIOUS PREVIEW OF THE COMING OF CHRIST ON THE LAST DAY!!

CROSS BEARING -- Study that concept in the light of Jesus' WORD
            "Take up your cross" -- Mark 8:30ff; Luke 9:21ff.
      Would you consider sickness, misfortune, and other involuntary "crosses"
      examples of what Jesus means by "Take up your cross"?
      Consider the CROSS - BEARING of Jesus as compared to our crosses

Who are the really great people in the world? Study the concepts of humility
      and temptation according to Matthew 18:1-14; Mark 9:33-37; Luke 9:46-50

On Prayer and forgiveness -- admonition to the erring -- Matthew 18:15-35
      Should the church be more disciplined on disciplining?
      What about excommunication? Discuss the possibility of that practice
                              in the church today

Why did people "hate" Jesus? John 7:1-52
      How do people express their hatred of Jesus today?

JESUS, THE VINE --- Are you drawing on the strength that comes from JESUS, THE VINE?

The beginning of a long argument -- John 8:1-30
      The remaining chapters of the Gospel of St.John tell the story of Jesus
      continual harassment from the Pharisees which ultimately ends in crucifixion.
      Read the remaining chapters of John in one setting before going on to the
      discussion of the individual incidents.

****

BIBLE READING GUIDE
for BIBLE READING PEOPLE

June 24 - Free indeed or FREE INDEED!   John 8:31-59; Luke 9:51-56

  25 - Real Dedication   Matthew 8:19-22;Luke 9:57-62;10:1-24

  26 - Who and what is really important?   Luke 10:25-42

  27 - Why sickness? -- Why healing?   John 9:1-41

June 28 - The Best Shepherd Around   John 10:1-21

     29 - What does it take   John 10:22-42; Luke 11:1-13
         to make you believe

     30 - Warnings of woe   Luke 11:14-54

****

REFLECTIONS ON READINGS

June 24 through June 30

A GREAT PROCLAMATION OF FREEDOM -- John 8:31-59
       What do you think Jesus meant by His statement of vs. 32?
           "THE TRUTH SHALL SET YOU FREE"
       How do we experience the freedom that Jesus talks about?
       Compare John 8:51 with John 6:29
           Is Jesus talking about obedience to the commandments?
           Or is He talking about the obedience of believing?
                     the obedience of faith?
       Consider Abraham's faith in the light of Romans 4:1-5
           Was Abraham saved by obedience to law or by obedience of faith?
       Consider the phrase "I AM" -- John 8:59; Compare Exodus 3:14

Why sickness? -- Why healing?
       Study carefully the account of John 9:1-41
       Compare the sickness and healing of Job --
       Review pages 6 & 7 of this Reading Guide concerning "Sickness and Suffering
       Compare Jeremiah 12:1-2

Consider the source of greatest gladness? -- Luke 10:1-20 (especially vs.20)

Consider the age old question -- "Who is my neighbor" -- Luke 10:25-42

Study the great lessons on "Shepherding" -- John 10
       Look once more for the "I Am's" -- All three of them

Great lessons on prayer -- Luke 11:13
       Compare Luke 11:9 with Revelation 3:20

Awesome demands and awful warning -- Luke 11:14-54
       WHAT DOES IT TAKE TO MAKE A PERSON BELIEVE??

****

BIBLE READING GUIDE
       for BIBLE READING PEOPLE

July 1 - Trusting in prosperity --   Luke 12:1-34
         or in PROVIDENCE

     2 - Are you ready??   Luke 12:35-59; 13:1-5

     3 - Puzzling things about the kingdom   Luke 13:6-15

July 4 - A lesson in liberty -- "Whosoever   Luke 14:1-35
         humbleth himself shall be exalted"

    5 - Lost sheep-lost coins-lost sons   Luke 15:1-32

    6 - Lessons on being fair -- and rich   Luke 16:1-31

    7 - Rebuking and repenting   Luke 17:1-10

****

REFLECTIONS ON READINGS

July 1 through July 7

Great lessons from Doctor Luke -- Physician of body and soul
      On guard about hypocrisy -- Luke 12:1-3
      Whom shall we fear? ------- Luke 12:4-7
      Compare Psalm 27; Psalm 46; and Romans 8:18-39

THE ONLY UNFORGIVABLE SIN -- The sin against the Holy Spirit -- Luke 12:8-11

Prosperity's danger -- Luke 12:22-34
      Compare Proverbs 30:7-9

A hard lesson to learn -- "Don't worry" -- Luke 12:22-34
      Discuss the problems of Vs. 33 -- Is it to be taken literally?
                                        Or does God have another meaning?

Are you ready for the coming? -- Luke 12:35-40

Discuss the obedience/disobedience concepts of Luke 12:41-48

Jesus the cause of division? -- Luke 12:49-53

Which way is the wind blowing -- Luke 12:54-56

Should believers hang there "dirty linen" in public? -- Luke 12:57-59
      Compare I Corinthians 6:1ff.
REPENTANCE -- How important is it? Luke 13:1-5

More Lessons from Doctor Luke
      The patience of GOD -- Luke 13:6-9
      Blue laws and Sabbath laws -- vs. 10-15
      Parables of faith   -------- vs. 18-21
      Open the door -- PLEASE ---- vs. 22-30
            Compare John 10:7 & 9
      Jesus great love for Jerusalem vs.31-35 --
            Does He love our cities less?
      Lessons on healing ----- Luke 14:1-6
      Humility --- Vs. 7-14
      Witnessing -- Vs. 15-24
      Does it cost to be a disciple? -- Luke 14:25-35
      A lesson on Christian management principles -- Luke 16:1-13

Lessons of Dr. Luke continued;
  On Divorce -- Luke 16:14-18
  For a full perspecive study the following:
    The major marriage principle -- Genesis 2:19-24
    Are there exceptions? -- Matthew 19:1-12; 5:31ff; Mark 10:1-11
                                 Luke 16:18; I Corinthians 7:1-39
    What are the exceptions- Matthew 19:9; I Corinthians 7:13-15

What is the church's role in relating to marital problems, separation, and divorce?
  (Rate the following on a scale of 1-10)
  (0 -- strongly disagree -- 10 stronly agree)

_____Reassert the major marriage principle -- "Til death do us part!"
_____Pronounce judgment for the wrong
_____Pronounce judgment with attending condemnation
_____Refuse communion unless there is reconciliation
_____Excommunicate both parties
_____Determine the innocent party and excommunicate the guilty party
_____Lead and counsel in confession an;d pronounce absolution
_____Keep hands off -- Don't interfere
_____Pronounce forgiveness and help people pick up the pieces and proceed
        with life -- Making the best of the circumstance remaining
_____Give continued blessing, counsel, and follow-up and share the
        fellowship in Jesus Christ

State any other opinions that may come to your mind.

LEARNING TO REPENT AND TO FORGIVE --- Luke 17:1-4

      JESUS SAYS , "if your brother sins, rebuke him,
                    if he repents, forgive him --
                    but we neither rebuke nor forgive very well!"

  Our faith and our duty -- Luke 17:5-10

****

BIBLE READING GUIDE
    for BIBLE READING PEOPLE

July 8 - The paradox of dying -- yet living   John 11:1-46
          Dead -- but alive!

      9 - What will it be like when He comes   John 11:47-54; Luke 17:11-37

     10 - Pharisees -- Publicans   Matthew 19:1-12; Mark 10:1-12
          Partners in marriage   Luke 18:15-17

     11 - All of us children   Matthew 19:13-15; Mark 10:13-16
                                                  Luke 18:15-17

     12 - Riches and righteousness   Matt 19:16-30; Mark 10:17-31

July 13 –Getting it all by grace   matthew 20:1-16; Luke 18:18-30

   14 - Predicting crucifixion   Matthew 20:17-28; Mark 10:32-34
                                                Luke 18:31-34

****

REFELECTIONS ON READINGS

July 8 through July 14

PARADOX OF DYING, YET BEING ALIVE -- John 11:1-46
        The four categories of death and life:
            I - Physically alive -- Spiritually dead
            II - Physically alive -- Spiritually alive
            III - Physically dead -- Spiritually alive
            IV - Physically dead -- Spiritually dead
                    Discuss -- Share personal views

An interesting parallel to John 11-50 -- II Samuel 17:3

What are the spiritual implications of the healing story of Luke 17:11ff?
        Of the coming of the Kingdom -- Luke 17:20ff

When it is hardest to pray -- PRAY HARDEST -- 2 examples -- Luke 18:1-7; 9-17

Children are the best believers -- Matthew 19:13-15; Mark 10:13-16; Luke 18:15-17

The riches of righteousness is the best riches of all--Matthew 19:16-30;Mark 10:17-31
        From our perspective, GRACE IS NEVER FAIR! -- Matthew 20:1-16; Luke 13:18-30

Getting ready to die -- Jesus' way -- Matthew 20:17-28; Mark 10:32-34; Luke 18:31-34

****

BIBLE READING GUIDE
for BIBLE READING PEOPLE

July 15 - The blind begin to see   Matthew 20:29-34; Mark 10:35-52
                                                Luke 18:35-43

   16 - How conversion changes things   Luke 19:1-28

   17 - Coming in the name of the Lord --   Matthew 21:1-11; Mark 11:1-11
        ON THE BACK OF A DONKEY?   John 11:55-57; 12:1-8

   18 - Praising with palms   Matthew 21:12-17; Luke 19:29-44;
                                                John 12:12-19

   19 - Figs and fakes   Matthew 21:18-22; Mark 11:12-16
                                                Luke 19:45-48

   20 - Who's the authority around here?   Matthew 21:23-32; Mark 11:27-33
                                                Luke 20:1-8

   21 - Worthy tenants   Matthew 21:33-46

July 15 through July 21

When you see Jesus -- FOLLOW HIM!
     Discuss the miracle and its spiritual implications -- Matthew 20:29-34
        Mark 10:46-52; Luke 18:35-43

How conversion changes life's attitudes -- Luke 19:1-10

Are we using God's gifts to God's glory? -- Luke 19:11-27
     Analyze your spiritual gifts? How are you using them to God's glory?

The beginning of the end? -- No -- The beginning of the return to glory
     Jesus heads for Jerusalem and crucifixion
     Preparation -- John 11:55-57
     The Bethany Pre-Anointment -- John 12:1-8

What's money for? -- The servant's no greater than the master-- John 12:9-11
     Compare John 15:18ff.

Onward and upward -- into the city -- Matthew 21:1-11; Mark 11:1-11
                            Luke 19:28-40; John 12:12-19
     Incongruities of the Kingdom -- THE KING ON A DONKEY
     The King cries for the city and its destiny -- Luke 19:41-44
     Getting angry at the goings on in church -- Matthew 12:12-17;
                                 Mark 11:15-19; Luke 19:45-48
     How does Jesus show His authority in our lives today? Matthew 21:23ff
                                 Mark 11:27-33; Luke 20:1-40

Concerning children in worship -- consider the following:

"All organizations within the congregation should serve this one supreme and primary objective, the corporate worship of the Christian assembly. This is to be the highest objective of the Sunday School, the Christian Day School, the youth leagues, all societies of the church, and all meetings conducted under the banner of the church. A college president, Dr. Silas Evans, has a thought provoking comment on church attendance of children and young people: 'If your child is not strong enough to go to both Sunday school and church, then hurry and call a doctor or send for an ambulance! If the doctor says the child may attend only one of the two, then choose the church service! The center of Christianity is to be found in the divine service. Even though the words of the pastor are not understood, the atmosphere and the impressions are lastimg. Why should we complain that so many young people do not go to church? They have never gone. A habit of worship is hard to start at an age when other habits are already formed'"- Spiritual Power for Your Congregation"
                                        Rev. Carl Berner -- CPH

Can you tell a fake when you see one? Matthew 21:18-22; Mark 11:12-14; 20-26

If Jesus is the Authority, why not obey Him? Matthew 21:23-32; Mark 11:27-32

Of landlords and tenants: Look for the point of the parable
     Compare Matthew 21:42 with I Peter 2:4-10 and Ephesians 2:19-22

BIBLE READING GUIDE
    for BIBLE READING PEOPLE

July 22 - "I will send my beloved son"   Mark 12:1-12; Luke 20:9-19

        23 - Taxes and tribute money   Matthew 22:1-22; Mark 12:13-17;
                                                Luke 20:20-26

        24 - All about the resurrection   Matthew 22:23-33; Mark 12:18-27
                                                Luke 20:27-38

        25 - The greatest commandment   Matthew 22"34-46; Mark 12:28-44
                                                Luke 20:39-40

        26 - ONE MASTER - JUST JESUS   Matthew 23:1-39

        27 - Who gives the most?   Mark 12:38-44; Luke 20:45-47; 21:1-4

        28 - Signs of the times   Matthew 24:1-51

****

REFLECTIONS ON READINGS

July 22 through July 28

Taxation Problems -- Matthew 22:1-22; Mark 12:13-17; Luke 20:20-26
        Interesting comparisons -- I Samuel 8; Romans 13:1-7
        How do you determine:
                What you owe to God? -- What you owe to the government?

In the light of Matthew 22:23-33; Mark 12:18-27; Luke 20:27-40
        Discuss the "Family Reunion" concept of heaven --
                "You will see him/her -- your loved one -- in heaven"
                What is the real union -- reunion -- we should be looking for?

Are there some commandments that are more important than others?
                Matthew 22:34-40; Mark 12:28-34

Why waste time arguing with Jesus? If He's the authority let Him be God!
                Matthew 22:41-46; 23:1-39; Mark 12:35-37; Luke 20:41-44

Who are the great givers? -- Mark 12:38-42; Luke 21:1-4

Can you tell when Jesus is coming? Consider the signs of the times
                Matthew 24:1-51 -- Compare Isaiah 2:19

****

BIBLE READING GUIDE
    for BIBLE READING PEOPLE

July 29 - Endurance plus   Mark 13: 1-37

        30 - See -- The Son of Man is coming!   Luke 21:5-38

July 31 - Wise virgins and useful talents   Matthew 25:1-30

August 1 - THE GREAT DAY OF HIS COMING   Matthew 25:31-46; 26:1-5
    Mark 14:1-2; Luke 22:1-2

    2 - Wasted? ON JESUS??   Matthew 26-6-16; Mark 14:3-11
    Luke 22:3-6; John 12

    3 - We'd like to see Jesus!   John 12:20-50

    4 - The day before the crucifixion   Matthew 26:17-25; Mark 14:12-21
    Luke 22:7-13

****

REFLECTIONS ON READINGS

July 29 through August 4

Is the glory of the church in its buildings?
    Or in its people?
    Or in the awesome events of the presence of the Lord --
       and in the anticipation of His coming?
       Discuss your views in the light of Mark 13:1-7 and Luke 21:5-18

Two significant parables of great interest:
    Look for the point of the parable and its spiritual meaning --
    Foolish virgins - Matthew 25:1-13 -- Wise investors - Matthew 25:14-30

Discuss your anticipation of the GREAT DAY OF HIS COMING -- Matthew 25:31-46
    Compare with Ephesians 2:4-10 and Revelation 20:1-5
       Are there contradictions? -- If so, what are they? Discuss them

The enemies of Christ meet secretly to make plans to kill him --
       Matthew 26:1-5; Mark 14:1-2; Luke 22:1-2
       Are there corollaries in contemporary church life?
       Refer also to Matthew 26:14-16; Mark 14:10-11; Luke 22:3-6; John 12:9-11

Does the church in any way waste its money on Jesus? Matthew 26:6-13; Mark 14:3-9
                                  John 12:1-8

What does it take to "see" Jesus today? -- John 12:20-50
    A good reminder for every pastor in sermon preparation and delivery

****

BIBLE READING BUIDE
for BIBLE READING PEOPLE

August 5 - Dining before Dying   Matthew 26:26-29; Mark 14:22-26
    Luke 22:14-23: John 13:21-35
    I Corinthians 11:23-26

    6 - Who is really a great person?   Luke 22:24-30; John 13:1-20

August 7 - A cock cries -- A man lies   Matthew 26:31-55; Mark 14;27-31
                                               Luke 22:31-38; John 13:36-38

        8 - Don't be afraid-The future is yours   John 14:1-31

        9 - As the Father loves -- So LOVE   John 15:1-27

       10 - The Spirit Comforter -- From   John 16:1-33
            the Father -- Thru the Son

       11 - A prayer of the Son -- for all   John 17:1-26
            sons (and daughters) of the KING

****

REFLECTIONS ON READINGS

August 5 through August 11

Discuss the meaning of greatness in the light of Jesus teaching -- Luke 22:24-30
        Consider the foot-washing -- John 13:1-20 -- (While this is a ceremony
                instituted by Christ, it does not offer forgiveness of sins -- thus it
                it is not considered a Sacrament as are Baptism and the Lord's Supper

A prediction of denial - Matthew 26:31-35;Mark 14:27-31;Luke 22:31-38;John 13:36-38
        How seriously do we take this caution in our own living?

This portion of John (Chapters 14-17) is an interesting study of the close relationship of the three persons of the Godhead, Father, Son and Holy Spirit. Do we significantly stress the work of the 3 persons in our theology and in our spirit of
living? Give ample time for discussion of this very important doctrine.

****

BIBLE READING GUIDE
    for BIBLE READING PEOPLE

August 12 - A fitful prayer   Matthew 26:30-46; Mark 14:26-47
                                               Luke 22:39-46; John 18:1

       13 - BETRAYAL   Matthew 26:47-56; Mark 14:43-52
                                                Luke 22:47-53; John 18:2-11

       14 - EXAMINED and CROSS - EXAMINED   Matthew 26:57-68; John 18:12-23

       15 - DENIAL -- DENIAL -- DENIAL   Matthew 26:69-75; Mark 14:53-72
                                                Luke 22:54-65; John 18:15-18; 25-27

       16 - From Counsel to condemnation   Matthew 17:1-2; Mark 15:1-5;
                                                Luke 22:66-71;23:1-5;John 18:15-18

       17 - Remorse and suicide   Matthew 27:3-14; Acts 1:18-19

       18 - Release a criminal --   Matt 27:15-26; Mark 15:6-15
            CRUCIFY CHRIST   Luke 23:6-12

August 12 through August 18

The <u>WEEK THAT SHOOK THE WORLD</u> -- The betrayal and passion of our Lord Jesus Christ
    "Kiss of Death" - Matthew 26:47-56; Mark 14:43-52; Luke 22:47-53; John 18:2-11
        Discuss the variants in the four accounts
        e.g. - "Put your sword back in its place"
            "I have not lost even one" John 18:9
            "The falling to the ground" John 18:6
            "This is your hour to act" Luke 22:53
            "Is it with a kiss that you betray?" Luke 22:48
            "The Scriptures must come true" Mark 14:49
            "Be quick about it, <u>friend</u>" Matthew 26:50
        Place these in contemporary circumstances -- What are the ways in which
           we personally and as a society betray Jesus?

Study the testimony of Jesus under interrogation -- Matthew 26:57-68; Mark 14:53-65;
                                       John 18:12-23
Historic denials - Matthew 26:69-75; Luke 22:54-62; Mark 14:66-72; John 18:15-27
        Contemporary: What are the ways in which we and people deny Jesus today?

From "church" judgment to civil condemnation -- Matthew 27:1-2; 11-14; Mark 15:1-5
                             Luke 22:66-71; 23:1-5; John 18:28-38
<u>Remorse</u> and <u>Suicide</u> -- JUDAS -- Matthew 27:3-10; Acts 1:18-19
        Isn't it strange that only Matthew describes the suicide of Jesus? -- Why?
        Discuss your views on suicide today --Its causes --Its problems --Its results

Release a criminal -- CRUCIFY JESUS -- Discuss injustices in today's court system?
                    Matthew 27:15-26; Mark 15:6-15; Luke 23:6-25

****

<u>BIBLE READING GUIDE</u>
    <u>for BIBLE READING PEOPLE</u>

August 19 - <u>MOCKERY</u> <u>DOUBLE JEOPARDY FOR JESUS</u>	Matthew 27:27-31; Mark 15:16-20 Luke 23:13-25; John 18:39-40;19:1-16
20 - BEAR YOUR OWN CROSS -- and HANG ON IT!	Matthew 27:32-44; Mark 15:21-32; Luke 23:26-32; John 19:28-37
21 - Words from the cross	Luke 23:33-43; John 19:18-27
22 - When the SON dies - it gets dark	Matthew 27:45-50; Mark 15:33-37 Luke 23:44-46; John 19:28-37
23 - The <u>BURIAL</u>	Matthew 27:51-61; Mark 15:38-47; Luke 23:47-56; John 19:38-42
24 - The <u>WATCH</u> -- The <u>WAITING</u> -- The <u>WONDER</u>	Matthew 27:62-66; 28:1-8; Mark 16:1-8
25 - <u>CHRIST APPEARS</u> -- <u>HE IS ALIVE!</u>	Matthew 28:9-15; Mark 16:9-11 Luke 24:1-12; John 20:1-10

<u>REFLECTIONS ON READINGS</u>

August 19 through August 25

"THE WEEK THAT SHOOK THE WORLD"

    The mockery of the court room -- Matthew 17:27-31;Mark 15:16-19;Luke 23:13-25
                     John 18:39-40; 19:1-16

    From the courtroom to the Cross- Matthew 27:32-44; Mark 15:20-32;
                     Luke 23:26-32; John 19:17

THE SEVEN WORDS OF THE SON OF GOD -- The dying Savior --

    Discuss the implication of each sentence spoken from the Cross

        1st Word -- "Father, forgive them..." -- Luke 23:34

        2nd Word -- "Today, you will be with me in Paradise" -- Luke 23:43

        3rd Word -- "Woman -- Son -- Mother"..--- John 19:27

        4th Word -- "My God! Why have you forsaken Me?" Matthew 27:46: Mark 15:34

        5th Word -- "I Thirst" -- John 19:28

        6th Word -- "It is finished" -- John 19:30

        7th Word -- "Into thy Hands, Father, I give my spirit" -- Luke 23:46

****

<u>BIBLE READING GUIDE</u>
    <u>for BIBLE READING PEOPLE</u>

August 26 - CHRIST APPEARS --   Mark 16:12-14; Luke 24:13-43
                                        John 20:19-25; I Corinthians 15:5

      27 - Fishing and feeding   John 20:26-29; John 21:1-24

      28 - You believe it?   Matthew 28:16-20; Mark 16:15-18
          GO TELL! -- GO TEACH!   Luke 24:44-49;Acts 1:3-8;I Cor.15:6-7

      29 - He is <u>COMING BACK</u>   Mark 16:19-20; Luke 24:50-53
                                          John 20:30-31; 21:25; Acts 1:9-;2

      30 - Resurrection to PENTECOST   Acts 1:1-2; 13-26

      31 - Surprising things of the spirit   Acts 2:1-47

September 1 Power and persecution   Acts 3:1-26

August 26 through Sepetember 1

Seen again and again -- AFTER THE RESURRECTION --

        By 2 disciples   -- Mark 16:12-13; Luke 24:13-35
        By 11 disciples -- Mark 16:14; Luke 24:36-46; John 20:19-22
        By Thomas   ------- A very special appearance -- John 20:24-31
        By disciples on the seashore, fishing -- John 21:1-25
                An ultimate question -- John 21:15
                An ultimate task ------ John 21:17;
                An ultimate invitation- John 21:19
        By more that 500 people at the same time -- I Corinthians 15:6-7

YOU BELIEVE IT? -- GO TELL IT! -- Matthew 28:16-20: Mark 16:15-17;
                                    Luke 24:47-49; Acts 1:9-12
        How active are you, and your church, in "telling it"? In what ways?

HE'S GONE, but very present -- AND COMING BACK -- Mark 16:19-20; Luke 24:50-53
        Consider what it will be like when He returns -- Acts 1:9-12

THE BEGINNING OF THE NEW ISRAEL

"I BELIEVE IN THE HOLY CHRISTIAN CHURCH" -- Its beginning at PENTECOST

        Surprising things of the Spirit -- Acts 2:1-47
        Discuss the ways in which the Holy Spirit is active in the Church today?
        Do today's struggles within the church reflect any progress from the past?
                Why or why not? -- Acts Chapter 3

****

BIBLE READING GUIDE
        for BIBLE READING PEOPLE

September 2 - In prison for Christ   Acts 4:1-31

        3 - Problems of community sharing   Acts 4:32-37; 5:1-11

        4 - The real test --   Acts 5:12-42
            Obeying God or obeying men

        5 - The Word of God increased   Acts 6

        6 - A stirring sermon --   Acts 7
            A tragic response

        7 - Exciting days   Acts 8

        8 - The SPIRIT confronts SAUL   Acts 9:1-25
            CHANGED --
            CONVERTED TO CHRIST

September 2 through September 8

As you read and study the Book of Acts, try to assess the questions:

    1 - What similarities do you find as you compare the Church <u>Then</u> and <u>NOW</u>?

    2 - What are the differences in the Church <u>THEN</u> and <u>NOW</u>?

Acts 4 - Discuss the "boldness" as reflected in this chapter of Acts.
       Discuss the doctrine of salvation as witnessed by Peter -- Vs.8-12
       Discuss the power of the Spirit in the lives of people -- <u>THEN</u> AND <u>NOW</u>
       Discuss the IDEAL Christian community -- Vs. 32-37
         Is such an arrangement possible today? -- Why? or Why not?

Acts 5 - What happens to the IDEAL when you deal with the "REAL" human situation
       Discuss the miracles, and the boldness, and the healings -- Vs.12-42
       Discuss religion in the <u>home</u> and in the <u>temple</u> -- Then and Now --

Acts 6 - Discuss the elements of Stephen's character --
       and other workers "full of the Holy Spirit"
       Compare "they prayed and placed their hands upon them" with the
         laying on of hands in the rite of ordination or a healing service

Acts 7 - Discuss this great sermon of Stephen -- Did he "win" or "lose"?

Acts 8 - Take note of the different places and procedures of baptism
       as it develops in the early church

Acts 9 - Study the circumstances of Saul/Paul as he is converted by the power
       of the Gospel and influence of the Holy Spirit

****

BIBLE READING GUIDF
    for BIBLE READING PEOPLE

September 9 - Paul & Peter --   Galatians 1:17-19; Acts 9:26-43
           Powerful in the Spirit

        10 - Cornelius, a Gentile   Acts 10
            converts to Christ

        11 - The early church gets going   Acts 11

        12 - A <u>MAN</u> puts his faith   Acts 12:1-2; James 1
            where his mouth is

        13 - Faith and works   James 2

        14 - Getting rid of sins that cripple James 3 and 4

        15 - The poor rich and the rich poor James 5

REFLECTIONS ON READINGS

September 9 through September 15

Discuss Paul's witness in Galatians 1:17-19

Talk about Peter's witness -- Acts 9:32-42; -- Cornelius Conversion Acts 10:1-43

Discuss Gentile/Jewish relationships as they existed then -- Acts 10:44-48--and now

Discuss -- "Baptized with the Holy Spirit" -- Acts 11:1-18; Review Acts 1:8

Believers now called <u>Christians</u> for the first time
    Discuss the persecution of the early Christians -- Acts 11:19-30; 12:1-2

The <u>TEACHINGS OF JAMES</u> -- Discuss the following:
    The relation of: -- Faith and Wisdom -- James 1:1-8; 3:13-18
                  Poverty and riches- --- 1:9-11; 5:1-6
                  Testing and tempting --- 1:12-18
                  Hearing and doing ----- 1:19-26; 2:1-13

    The problem of prejudice -- James 2:1-13
    The temptation of tongue-talk -- James 3:1-12
    The three-fold enemy (Luther) The DEVIL, the WORLD, our FLESH -- James 4:1-11
    Patience and Prayer -- James 5:7-19
    A challenge to Courage -- James 5:20

****

BIBLE READING GUIDE
for BIBLE READING PEOPLE

September 16 - Released by an angel   Acts 12:3-25

      17 - Spiritually and physically blind Acts 13:1-13

      18 - Glad tidings -- Everywhere   Acts 13:;4-52

      19 - Itinerant preachers   Acts 14

      20 - Circumcision and conversion   Acts 15:1-2; Galatians 2:7-10

      21 - The argument is settled   Acts 15:13-41; Galatians 2:11-14

      22 - Strange places for conversions   Acts 16

****

REFLECTIONS ON READINGS

September 16 through September 22

In spite of what he said -- Did James deserve this? Acts 12:2
    But there are other people with the name James -- e.g. Acts 15:13

Peter is spared -- Acts 12:3-19
        The persecutor (Herod) is dead -- Acts 12:20-25

The beginnings of organized mission work --
        The Holy Spirit said, "GO" -- Acts 13
                To Cyprus -- To Antioch
        The message? -- "JESUS -- THE SAVIOR OF THE PEOPLE OF ISRAEL" Acts 13:23
        The Jews and the Gentiles come together in the church -- BELIEVERS IN JESUS
                Forgiveness of sin is preached to both -- Acts 13:39
                Some Jews reject Jesus -- Acts 13:45-48

The WORD goes to Iconium, Lystra, and Derbe -- and back to Antioch - Acts 14

A Church Convention -- Conflict on circumcision -- a fierce argument -- Acts 15
        "no difference between us" vs.9 -- A letter of compromise -- Acts 15:22-24
        But -- Another sharp argument -- Acts 15:36-41
        Discuss some of the major conflicts of the church today

MISSION WORK goes on
        Work in strange places results in conversions to Christ -- Acts 16
                "Down by the riverside"
                "Inside those prison walls"

****

BIBLE READING GUIDE
        for BIBLE READING PEOPLE

September 23 - Arguing "out" of Scripture --   Acts 17
                Not "about" Scripture

            24 - A real live church   Acts 18:1-17; I Thessalonians 1:1-10

            25 - Sharing the ministry   I Thessalonians 2 and 3

            26 - Goals for God   I Thessalonians 4 and 5

            27 - Watch out! False teachers   II Thessalonians 1 and 2

            28 - Pray for us   II Thessalonians 3; Acts 18:18-22

            29 - Dispersing the confusion   Acts 18:23-28; Acts 19:1-41

****

REFLECTIONS ON READINGS

September 23 through September 29

"JESUS IS THE MESSIAH -- Acts 17:3
        If you want to convince people -- know your Scriptures -- Acts 17:2
        The jealous Jews jeopardize Jason -- Acts 17:5-9
        Have you ever been harassed because of your faith? Talk about it
        How can we develop a more courageous witness?

Take a lesson from the Bereans -- Acts 17:3

"Everyday they studied the Scriptures"

A sermon to the intelligentsia of the University of Athens -- Acts 17:16-34

Does the church do an adequate job of reaching the educated people today?
Discuss the ways and means that we try to reach our college campuses

The theme of the mission work at Corinth -- "Jesus is the Messiah"
Why do you think Paul kept emphasizing the precise message?

Riots and resistance at Ephesus -- Acts 19

THEOLOGY FOR THESSALONIANS -- AND US!

A vibrant church -- Joy that comes from the Holy Spirit - I Thess. 1:1-10
Sharing the ministry -- I Thessalonians 2 and 3
Set some goals for God- I Thessalonians 4:1-11
The truth about the coming Jesus -- I Thessalonians 4:13 through 5:11
Final instructions -- I Thessalonians 5:12-28
Be happy - Be thankful - Follow the Spirit - Trust God's amazing grace

To eradicate confusion about Christ's coming, read and discuss --
II Thessalonians Chapters 1 - 2 - and 3

Back to the mission fields -- Acts 18:18-28; 19:1-41
Discuss the Holy Spirit and baptism
Share your views on the riots at Ephesus --
Does the proclamation of the Gospel cause unrest anywhere today? Why?

****

BIBLE READING GUIDE
for BIBLE READING PEOPLE

September 30 - Diuisions and trials   I Corinthians 1:1-31
in the early church

October   1 - The power of Spirit preaching   I Corinthians 2;1-16;3:1-23

2 - The need of faithful   I Corinthians 4:1-21; 5:1-13
leadership in the church

3 - Patterns for a proper church   I Corinthians 6:1-20

4 - Major marriage guidelines   I Corinthians 7:1-40

5 - A proper ministry   I Corinthians 8:1-13; 9:1-27
needs proper support

6 - Traditions abused --   I Corinthians 10:1-33
But reiterated

REFLECTIONS ON READINGS

September 30 through October 6

SOME INTRODUCTORY REMARKS TO THE READING OF CORINTHIANS
> If you belong to a congregation that is experiencing problems and conflicts
> Paul's letters to the congregation at Corinth will assure you that you are not
> alone. As you read Corinthians two things are of immense importance --
>
>> 1) Study the problem -- How similar are they to the problems experienced
>> by congregations of today?
>>
>> 2) Study the solution - What does God's Word say that will be helpful in
>> solving the problems in the contemporary church

Problems and the Power of the Gospel -- I Corinthians 1:1-31

God's wisdom and human wisdom in contrast -- I Corinthians 2:1-16
> Note particularly the need for the Spirit's enlightenment
> Review in this context the 3rd Article and meaning from Luther's Catechism
> Are pastors called to be popular or proclaimers of Christ and builders
>> of the church -- (God's spiritual temple -- Vs. 9-10) Discuss
> When will the true faithfulness of God's servants be revealed? I Cor.4:9-23

Do you think sexual immorality a new problem? -- Study I Corinthians 5
> Compare I Corinthians 5;12-13 with Matthew 7:1-6

Where do christians go to solve their legal disputes? -- Study I Corinthians 6:1-6

Take good care of your body -- it's the Temple of the Holy Spirit -- I Cor. 6:19

Discuss this very important question and apply to our current conditions --
> Can worshipers of idols (what's an idol?), or adulterers, or homosexual
> perverts, or stealers, or greedy people, or drunkards, or slanderers
> be saved? -- Read carefully I Corinthians 6:9-11
> REMEMBER ---- As we study the problems of obvious sins that none of us are
>> saved because we are <u>less guilty</u> than others -- Whoever we are
>> <u>WE ARE SAVED BY GRACE "without any merit or worthiness in us"</u>

A MAJOR PRINCIPAL - Work with evangelical persuasion -- Consider our sins as we
> apply Law and Gospel to our own lives and the lives of others

Marriage problems - Study I Corinthians 7 for guidance and help

The problem of <u>offense making</u> and <u>offense taking</u> -- I Corinthians 8

Giving the ministry proper support -- I Corinthians 9
> Everything for the Gospel's sake -- 9:23
> As an athlete trains, so every christian trains to be in shape -- I Cor.9:23-27

<u>"WHATEVER YOU DO - DO IT ALL TO GOD'S GLORY"</u> -- I Corinthians 10:31
> None of us does that perfectly -- The Law of God reminds us of that daily
> We are saved by grace -- Thank God the Holy Gospel of God reminds us
> of that daily as well.-- In perspective consider Romans 7:15-20 and 7:25
>> Study also Philippians 3:13 and with Paul "keep striving"

BIBLE READING GUIDE
         for BIBLE READING PEOPLE

October 7 - Guidance and guidelines   I Corinthians 11:1-34; 12:1-31
                for christian service

        8 - The greatest gift -- LOVE   I Corinthians 13:1-13; 14:1-40

        9 - GOSPEL and RESURRECTION   I Corinthians 15:1-58

       10 - Good instructions and   I Corinthians 16:1-24; I Timothy 1:3
            motives for ministry   II Corinthians 1:1-24; Acts 20:1

       11 - Triumphant ministry   II Corinthians 2:1-17; 3:1-18

       12 - Suffering and dying   II Corinthians 4:1-18; 5:1-21

       13 - Set-backs and separation   II Corinthians 6:1-18; 7:1-16

****

REFLECTIONS ON READINGS

October 7 through October 13

Guidance and guidelines for Corinthians -- and US

        1 - WORSHIP -- Discuss the context of I Corinthians 11:1-16
                       Women's role in worship

        2 - THE LORD'S SUPPER -- I Corinthians 11:17-34 -- Who should or should not
                                 participate in this fellowship meal

        3 - THE GIFTS OF THE SPIRIT -- I Corinthians 12 -- Use the gifts to the glory
                                       of Christ and for the benefit of the Church

ALL YOU WANT TO KNOW ABOUT LOVE -- I Corinthians 13:1-13
        Is this to be treated as Law or Gospel? Discuss
        Putting love into practce -- using God's gifts -- I Corinthians 14:1-25
        Using love in worship -- I Corinthians 14:26-40; Compare I Corinthians 11:1-34

THE POWERFUL MESSAGE OF RESURRECTION -- I Corinthians 15
        The centrality of CHRIST's resurrection -- vs.1-11
        The focus of our own resurrection -------- vs.12-58

GUIDANCE FOR GIVING: Consider "Paul"s Pod of P's"
        Give Periodically ------ I Corinthians 16:2 -- the first day of the week
        Give Personally -------- I Corinthians 16:2 -- each one of you
        Give Proportionately --- I Corinthians 16:2 -- From what you have earned
        Give Preservingly ------ I Corinthians 16:2 -- save it up
        Give Purposefully ------ I Corinthians 16:2 -- no need for special collections
Plans for God"s servants -- THE PASTORS -- I Corinthians 16:5-12
        Support God's leaders -- men and women -- I Corinthians 16:13-20
        In conclusion -- strong message of LAW -- and GOSPEL __ vs.22-24
        Compare I Timothy 1:3 and Acts 20:1

-160-

II CORINTHIANS -- Two years later -- 57 A.D.
        Confidence in suffering - Thanksgiving for deliverance - II Corinthians 1:1-12
        No pleasing platitudes -- Only firmness in the Gospel -- II Corinthians 1:13-24
        Forgiveness and victory - Through union with Christ -- II Corinthians 2:
        Credentials for serving in the New Testament time -- II Corinthians 3:
        The mix of humanity in persons (common clay pots) -- But divinely called to
                high purpose in serving -- II Corinthians 4
                "We speak because we believe"
        Prepared to live on -- IN CHRIST -- II Corinthians 5:1-10
        A purpose for living - IN CHRIST -- II Corinthians 5:11-21
        The paradox of life for the Lord's called servant -- II Corinthians 6
                Attacked and defended -- Honored and disgraced -- Insulted and praised--
                Accused as liars but speaking the truth -- Unknown but known -- Dead but
                alive -- Sad, but glad -- Poor but rich --
                Having nothing but possessing everything
                Sadness over sin leads to joy of salvation

****

BIBLE READING GUIDE
    for BIBLE READING PEOPLE

October 14 - The grace of giving   II Corinthians 8:1-24; 9:1-15

        15 - Self-esteem   II Corinthians 10:1-18; 11:1-33
             in ministerial authority

        16 - Effective service   II Corinthians 12:1-21; 13:1-14
             through honest relationship

        17 - The glory of the Gospel   Acts 20:2-3; Galatians 1:1-25; 2:1-6

        18 - Saved by faith --   Galatians 2:15-21; 3:1-29
             freed from condemnation

        19 - Adopted in sonship   Galatians 4:1-31
             with Jesus Christ

        20 - The application of grace   Galatians 5:1-26; 6:1-18
             in christian living

****

REFLECTIONS ON READINGS

October 14 through October 20

Talk about giving -- Look at the Corinthians -- What an example -- II Cor. 8 and 9

The self-defense of self-esteem -- for pastors who need it -- II Cor. 10 and 11

A vision of paradise -- II Corinthians 12:1-6 -- But a special burden -- vs.7-10

Problems in human relationships -- II Corinthians 12:11-21

The basis of relationship in the christian congregation -- II Corinthians 13
     The power of Christ's death and resurrection

HOW GREAT THE GOSPEL TO BE PROCLAIMED -- Acts 20:2-3; Galatians 1 & 2:1-6

Is there any evidence of FALSE GOSPEL in our day and age?
     Compare Galatians 1:6-23 and Galatians 2:1-5
     Building on law or building on faith -- Galatians 2:6-21 and Galatians 3
     Christians by adoption -- not by physical birth -- Galatians 4:1-6

A falling out between the pastor and the people -- Galatians 4:8-20

Mt.Sinaii and Mt.Calvary in stark contrast -- Galatians 4:21-31

The grace of God leads to freedom of NEW LIFE in Christ -- Galatians 5
     No longer a bondage to human nature (Old Adam)
     Compare Paul's spirit as reflected in Galatians 6:1 with II Cor.10:4-6
     Sharing burdens and doing good -- Galatians 6

****

BIBLE READING GUIDE
     for BIBLE READING PEOPLE

October 21 - Ready to preach   Romans 1:1-32

       22 - The terrible tribulation   Romans 2:1-29
            of the impenitent

       23 - ALL lost in sin -- Saved by faith   Romans 3:1-31

       24 - Back to basics   Romans 4:1-25

       25 - By one man (Adam) sin --   Romans 5:1-21
            by one man (Jesus) salvation

       26 - Raised to new response-ability   Romans 6:1-23; 7:1-6

       27 - Discovering the enemy --ME   Romans 7:7-15

****

REFLECTIONS ON READINGS

October 21 through October 27

The beautiful BOOK OF ROMANS
     As Isaiah is the heart of Old Testament theology, so Romans is the
     heart of theolgy in the New Testament -- A corollary book to read --
     "How to be a Christian Without Being Religious" - Ridenor - Regal Books

Chapter 1 - Look for the accents of Christology -- Who is Jesus?
             Look for LAW/GOSPEL delineations
             Remember these premises as you proceed with Romans

Chapter 2 - Is God justified in being angry? Explain
          Study the contrast of vs.6-16 with 3:9-26
          Who are the real Israelites in New Testament theology -- Vs. 28-29
          Watch for the developments of that theme in Romans 9 through 11

       3 - How do we abuse God's grace?
           The REAL ISSUE -- Are we saved by God's law or by God's grace?
                         By self-righteousness or Christ's righteousness

       4 - Were people of the Old Testament saved differently than those of the New?
           Abraham was saved by the MERCY OF God -- We are saved by the GRACE of God

       5 - Study the concept-- By one man's sin -- all sinners -- all condemned
                         By one man's perfecton -- all made perfect --

       6 - Study the imagery of baptism -- Immersed in CHRIST-- Raised to NEW LIFE
           What do you thing Paul means when he says, "We are dead to sin"? Vs.11
           Study the Law/Gospel content of vs.23

       7 - Study the psychological impact of Romans 7:14-25
           Study the imagery of marriage and the freedom of the Gospel -- vs.1-6

****

BIBLE READING GUIDE
     for BIBLE READING PEOPLE

October 28 - The real friend -- Jesus   Romans 8:1-39

        29 - The Jews and jesus   Romans 9:1-33

        30 - Confess Christ!   Romans 10:1-21; 11:1-36

        31 - LIVE for Christ --   Romans 12:1-21

November 1 - Living and dying in the Lord   Romans 14; and 15:1-14

         2 - Personalities in the church   Romans 15:15-53; 16:1-27

         3 - Going home   Acts 20:4-38

****

REFLECTIONS ON READINGS

October 28 through November 3

(Romans)
Chapter 8 - Contrast Paul's concept of human nature vs. new nature -- vs.1-17
          Study the tremendous concept of "suffering in time"
              As contrasted with the "glory that shall be revealed in us" vs.18-39

       9 - Study the concept -- "NOT ALL OF ISRAEL ARE OF ISRAEL" -- vs.6
           This has much to say about the NEW ISRAEL!
           All believers in Christ (New Israel) are also THE HOLY CHRISTIAN CHURCH

-163-

Chapter 9 - What do you think of God's challenge -- "Don't get smart with Me?"
Are all Jews going to be saved? -- vs. 27

10 - How does the Word of God get around? -- vs.14-17
and 11 - Who are the small group of Jews to be saved? 11:1-12
How does this effect the Gentile world? vs.13ff.
Cast in this light -- Who now is "all Israel"? vs.26
Read the Doxology out loud -- vs.33-36

14 - The real purpose of Scripture -- 15:4-6
and 15 - The boldness needed to preach the Word --vs. 14-21

18 - Fraternity in the Fellowship

Back to the history and the development of the early church -- Acts 20
A touching sermon -- vs. 17-18
What important messages are accented in the sermon?
What about the emotions displayed?

****

BIBLE READING GUIDE
for BIBLE READING PEOPLE

November 4 - Persecuted for preaching	Acts 21:1-40
5 - A changed and converted man	Acts 22:1-30
6 - Entrapment	Acts 23:1-35
7 - Confessions in court	Acts 24:1-23; 25:1-27
8 - Almost a conversion	Acts 26:1-32
9 - Set sail again	Acts 27:1-44
10 - "Snake bit"	Acts 28:1-16

****

REFLECTIONS ON READINGS

November 4 through November 10

Study the concept of the Holy Spirit giving conflicting directions to Paul and the
people of Tyre -- Acts 20:22-24; 21:4 & 11-12

The way of the committed disciple--"If they persecute me -- They will persecute you"
Compare John 15:18ff with Acts 21
A dramatic change in a converted man -- Acts 22
Think of some contemporary corollaries to Paul's conversion
A serious confrontation with argumentative words -- Acts 23
A christian disciple on trial in a civil court -- Acts 24
Study the intrigue and innuendo of the prosecution--the defense and the judge
On to the supreme court -- Acts 25

Consider and discuss the evangelistic witness of Paul -- Acts 26
        And the responses of the other people -- e.g. Festus -- vs.24
        Literal -- from the Greek -- "In a little, me you persuade to be a Christian?"
        Is that sarcasm or is it an earnest confession?
        On to the high court at Rome -- Acts 27
Ill winds -- Ill tempers -- and a shipwreck -- Acts 27
        "Snake bit!" -- Acts 28:1-10
        The WITNESS -- the result -- Some believed, some disagreed -- Acts 28:11-30
                Compare this with contemporary situations

****

BIBLE READING GUIDE
    for BIBLE READING PEOPLE

November 11 - interceding for a friend   Philemon 1:1-25; Colossians 1:1-29
               and fellow in the faith

        12 - Walking upright --   Colossians 2:1-23; 3:1-25
             with a risen Christ

        13 - Continuing in prayer   Colossians 4:1-18

        14 - The real meaning of faith   Ephesians 1:1-23; 2:1-22

        15 - The CHURCH and NEW LIFE   Ephesians 3:1-21; 4:1-32

        16 - Strong in the faith   Ephesians 5:1-33; 6:1-24

****

REFLECTIONS ON READINGS

November 11 through November 16

Philemon -- Just one chapter -- Study the perspective of the human relationships
            involved in a forgiven slave -- but also a christian brother
Colossians- Great words -- GRACE AND PEACE
            What do they really mean? -- 1:2ff.
            Thank God for God's people - 1:3-9
            What is the real purpose of our lives? -- 1:9-29
            What a full life in Christ is all about! -- Chapters 2 and 3
            Some good instructions for very practical relationships -- Chapter 4
Ephesians - What is God's plan for His world -- 1:1-14
            Study the perspectives of Paul's prayer -- vs.15-23
            From death to life -- Chapter 2
            Try to define, illustrate if possible, the meaning of grace--vs.8-10
            How do we put into practice our one-ness in Christ --
                    With people who are different? vs.11-22
            How do those in the body of Christ display their unity in Christ? Ch.3&4
            What is the job of the "called" -- The servants of the Lord?
                    (full-time church workers) -- 4:11-16
            Very practical instructions for christian living:
                    Avoid Satan -- follow the Spirit -- Chapter 4 - 6

BIBLE READING GUIDE
    for BIBLE READING PEOPLE

November 17 - Confident in Christ   Philippians 1:1-30

        18 - Serving the exalted Christ   Philippians 2:1-30; 3:1-15

        19 - The believer's Strength   Philippians 4:1-23

        20 - Some believed -- Some did not!   Acts 28:17-31

        21 - Dangerous doctrines   I Timothy 1:1-20; 2:1-15

        22 - The office of the ministry   I Timothy 3:1-16; 4:1-16

        23 - The work of the minister   I Timothy 5:1-25; 6:1-21
****

REFLECTIONS ON READINGS

November 17 through November 23

Philippians - A beautiful letter of encouragement to any Christian congregation.
              To live IN CHRIST is to love life now, here and forever --
              Study Paul's discourse on the tensions of living or dying-Chap.1:20-26
              How does Paul answer the question "What is life?" vs. 21ff
                  Apply that to "Identity Crises" or "Finding one's self"
              Study the Christology as expressed in Chapter 2
              How do we attain true righteousness? Chapter 3
              Are we ready to discipline ourselves in the style of Paul's analogy
                  of the athlete? What could you do to improve your spiritual health?
              Tender feelings towards faithful friends and co-workers - Chapter 4

I Timothy
        Paul in Rome -- Effective instructions to a young minister --
        Warnings about dangerous doctrines -- I Timothy 1:1-11
        What is the current attitude in the church and society about DOCTRINE?
        Study Chapter I in the context of proper distinction of Law and Gospel
        Proper conduct for church worship -- Chapter 2
        What kind of leaders do you really want? -- Chapter 3
        How to be a good servant of Jesus Christ -- Chapters 4 - 6
        Would you like to be a minister? Have you encouraged some young person
            you know to study for full time work in the church?

****

BIBLE READING GUIDE
    for BIBLE READING PEOPLE

November 24 - Elders in the church   Titus:11-16; 2:1-15; 3:1-15

        25 - Christians get hurt   I Peter 1:1-25; 2:1-25
             Christ, too, suffered injustice

        26 - Christianity in marriage   I Peter 3:1-22; 4:1-19

November 27 - Stand strong -- FAREWELL   I Peter 5:1-14

        28 - Of prophets and angels   Hebrews 1:1-14; 2:1-18

        29 - A heavenly calling   Hebrews 3:1-19; 4:1-16

        30 - The high, HIGH PRIEST   Hebrews 5:1-14; 6:1-20

****

REFLECTIONS ON READINGS

November 24 through November 30

TITUS-The character and responsibility of an elder
        In temperament-Chapter 1; In doctrine-2; In conduct-3
        Study the effect of the Holy Spirit's intervention on one's life -- 3;3-7

I PETER --- A powerful message for then and now
            Great losses offset by great promises -- 1:1-12
            The call to a great life in Christ -- 1:13-25
            Our great calling as christians -- 2:1-17
            How to endure injustice when it happens for the cause of Christ-2:18-24
            Instructions for right living -- Chapters 3 and 4
                "The end of all things is near"
                Does this have any effect on your attitude toward life? -- Discuss
            "Shepherds of the flock" -- what to watch for -- Chapter 5
                Hold on 'til glory time -- 5:10
            Being alert to the real work of the church -- 5:1-14
                What kind of shepherding do you experience in your "flock"?

HEBREWS --- The Book of Hebrews represents the closest touch of the New Testament
            message with that of the Old Testament. As you read you will recall
            much of the Old Testament worship and sacrificial ritual that we read
            about in the first two years of this series. Watch for the comparisons
            God's Word comes through prophets and angels -- the exultation of Christ
                Hebrews 1:1-14 -- Compare Psalm 8; also Psalm 29
            Study the Christology of Chapter 2
            Jesus and Moses -- Assess the comparison of the two -- Chapter 3
                Are the warnings still applicable today? -- vs. 12-19
            God's promise and God's Word -- Look for nuances of LAW/GOSPEL in Chap.4
            The work of Christ as priest compared with Melchizedek -- 4:15-5:14
                Compare Genesis 14:17
            GROW UP -- CHRISTIAN! -- 6:1-20

****

BIBLE READING GUIDE
    for BIBLE READING PEOPLE

December 1 - JESUS CHRIST -- A Priest forever   Hebrews 7:1-28

        2 - The full and final sacrifice   Hebrews 8:1-13; 9:1-28

        3 - ONE offering for sin FOREVER   Hebrews 10:1-39

December 4 - <u>BY FAITH BY FAITH BY FAITH</u>   Hebrews 11:1-40

      5 - The WALK and the WORSHIP   Hebrews 12:1-29
          of the believer

      6 - Look for the city to come   Hebrews 13:1-25

      7 - Get stirred up -- IN THE FAITH   II Peter 1:1-21

      8 - Signs and signals of apostasy   II Peter 2:1-22
****

REFLECTIONS ON READINGS

December 1 through December 8

Study the difference between: -- Melchizadek (the human priest) and
                             CHRIST (the divine priest) Hebrews 7 through 8:13
Can God ever forget? -- Hebrews 8:12 -- Compare Jeremiah 31:34
     Discuss the implication of that in our lives --
     In that perspective compare the nature of God with our nature

Discuss the implications of earthly and heavenly worship as described in Hebrews 9
     How does Christ become the ultimate and final sacrifice? -- Hebrew 10
     Why do we make "sacrifices and offerings"?

The GIANTS of faith -- Chapter 11
     How can we learn from their examples?
     Compare the life of Job and our own suffering in the light of Hebrews 12
     Don't get to attached to earthly "cities" -- They won't last --
          LOOK FOR THE CITY TO COME -- The New Jerusalem -- Which is heaven!
<u>II PETER</u> -- Discuss the concept of a truly devoted life -- II Peter 1:1-21
        Are we aware of the apostosy in our lives and the lives of others?
          As Peter describes them? -- II Peter 2
****

<u>BIBLE READING GUIDE</u>
   <u>for BIBLE READING PEOPLE</u>

December 9 - Promises fulfilled   II Peter 3:1-18
         in the worst of times

      10 - Hope in the face of hopelessness   Jude 1:1-25

      11 - Good soldiers of Jesus Christ   II Timothy 1:1-18; 2:1-26

      12 - Signs of the last times   II Timothy 3:1-17; 4:1-22

      13 - The true way to joy   I John 1:1-10; 2:1-14

      14 - How surprising and surpassing   I John 2:15-29; 3:1-24
          is the LOVE OF GOD

      15 - Where LOVE had its beginning   I John 4:1-21

December 9 through December 15

The integrity of a sound marital relationship -- Do the modes of relationship of
           husband and wife today fit that Scriptural pattern? -- II Peter 3:1-7
           Compare Paul's instruction -- Ephesians 5:21ff

"Being A Christian When The Chips Are Down" -- II Peter 3:8-22; I Peter 4:12ff
        Rescource reading -- Helmut Thielicke -- Fortress Press, Philadelphia

"The end of all things is near" -- II Peter 4
      What effect does this message have on your attitude towards life?

Being alert to the real work of the church -- II Peter 5:1-14
        Discuss "shepherding" as it goes on in the church today
            In your congregation

JUDE -One small chapter with a mighty message --
       What do you make of the description of "good" and "evil" angels?
       Are the warnings of false prophets appropriate to today's church?

II TIMOTHY -
             Words of courage to a young pastor -- Chapters 1 & 2
             From his "Father in the faith" -- The Apostle Paul

             Instructions for the "last days"- II Timothy 3 & 4
             How do these words effect your spirit and fellowship with God's people?

I JOHN ---- Consider the following:

        1 - The beautiful assurance as to who Jesus really is -- 1:1-7
        2 - The power of personal confession -- 1:8-10
        3 - AND the power of ABSOLUTION!
           Compare the confession/absolution rite of the Lutheran Liturgy
           with this portion of Scripture -- Discuss its significance --
        4 - When the Holy Spirit is "poured out" on us what effect does that
           have on our faith and life? -- 2:1-29
        5 - Children of God in love with each other -- Chapter 3
        6 - The true and the false spirit as determined by our knowledge of
           where true love begins and how we get it and how we share it
           with each other -- Chapter 4 -- A most important chapter for the
           proper understanding of honest LAW/GOSPEL theology

       7 - THE ULTIMATE VICTORY -- Chapter 5

****

BIBLE READING GUIDE
    for BIBLE READING PEOPLE

December 16 - The power to overcome   I John 5:1-21; II John 1:1-13

      17 - The great joy   III John 1:1-14

****

REFLECTIONS ON READINGS

December 16 through December 23

II JOHN - Discuss the impact of the words "Peace be with you" in this context --

IIIJOHN - Personalities in the life of the church --
        Can you recognize contemporary acquaintances who would fit the
        characteristics of the following mentioned in III John?
        1 - Gaius -- 2-Diotrophes -- 3 - Demetruis -- Discuss

****

THE BOOK OF REVELATION -- THE GLORIOUS FINALE!!

As you read the Book of Revelation be aware that some of the keenest differences in
Biblical interpretation are apparent when you read much material pertaining to this
Book. There are two main schools of thought to take into consideration:

     1 - The fundamentalist interpretation which seeks to make literal
        the prophecies of Revelation and make direct application to
        the fulfillment of those prophecies in current happenings

     2 - Those who follow the "Apocalyptic" approach, who see "The
        Apocalypse", (as THE REVELATION is often called), as a Book of
        figurative images portraying the greater scene of the whole New
        Testament era, symbolized in pictures portraying the battle of Christ
        with Satan, culminating in the victory of the King of Kings and
        Lord of Lords, who then rules through all eternity

The Lutheran Church, along with many others, generally follows the latter course of
Biblical interpretation. (See "Apocalyptic Prophecy" -- from "Interpreting the Holy
Scripture" -- Dr. Herbert Mayer -- Concordia Publishing House - St.Louis, Mo.

Analyze, as you proceed through the first three chapters, the special descriptions
of the seven churches of Asia Minor. Picture your congregation in your mind.
Compose a letter that you think would describe your congregation through the eyes of
the Holy Spirit. Share that letter with those around you as John shared his.

Visualize in your mind that you are the Apostle John receiving the visions of Chapters 4 and 5. What interpretation would you place on these visions.?

Follow the same mental process with Chapter 6 concerning the seals.

Sometime during the course of your reading of the Book of Revelation obtain a recording (or attend a concert during the Christmas season) of Handel's grand oratorio "THE MESSIAH". Remember and contemplate the inspired words of John's Revelation as you listen to the "HALLELUJAH CHORUS". What fascinating joy we experience as we read and listen.

Read Chapter 7 slowly and let your mind sink into deep contemplation

Mentally and spiritually fasten your meitative attention to the great scenes
        of Chapters 8 & 9

****

BIBLE READING GUIDE
        for BIBLE READING PEOPLE

December 24 - Mysteries of God   Revelation 9:1-21; 10:1-11
              exposed in visions

        25 - The grand temple of eternity   Revelation 11:1-19; 12:1-17
             (Read the Christmas story)   Luke 2:1-20

        26 - Blessed to die --   Revelation 13:1-18; 14:1-20
             to live forever

        27 - Blessings and blasphemy   Revelation 15:1-8; 16:1-21

        28 - The LAMB OF GOD   Revelation 17:1-18; 18:1-24
                iS LORD OF LORDS
                    and KING OF KINGS

        29 - The marriage of heaven   Revelation 19:1-21

        30 - The grand and glorious   Revelation 20:1-15; 21:1-27
                NEW JERUSALEM

        31 - For this -- COME QUICKLY --   Revelation 22:1-21
                LORD JESUS

****

REFLECTIONS ON READINGS

December 24 through December 31

Contemplate the final instructions of Chapter 10 -- particularly vs. 11
    Do we take that seriously for our day? Why? or Why not?

Where and how do you see the works of Satan described in Chapter 11?
    The work of Christ? vs. 15ff.
    Compare vs. 19 with Ephesians 2:20ff and Exodus 25

Would you agree that possibly the woman of Revelation 12:1-6 is the Virgin Mary?
    What other possiblities present themselves? Use a commentary for reference

Compare Revelation 12:11 with the Book of Jude

How do Christians fit into the picture of Revelation 12:17?

Compare Matthew 20:15-16; & Matthew 22:14 with Revelation 13, particularyly vs.5-10

Are you ready to sing the NEW SONG of Revelation 14 & 15?

Compare Revelation 16 with the judgment scene of Matthew 25:31ff.

Whom do you visualize the famous "prostitute" to be? -- Revelation 17

    Who is the "Great Babylon"? -- Revelation 17 and 18:1-3

Who are the people of Revelation 18:4-8; and 18:9-24

Contemplate the wedding scene of Chapter 19 -- Who is the lamb?
                           Who is the bride?

    Who is the "rider on the white horse"? - Revelation 19:11ff.

Compare the RESURRECTION SCENE of John 5:19-29

    with the RESURRECTION SCENE of Revelation 20:4-6

    Satan goes to Hell forever -- Revelation 20:7-15

NOW THE <u>NEW HEAVEN</u> -- THE NEW EARTH -- THE NEW JERUSALEM -- Revelation 21
    Who gets there and who doesn't? -- Revelation 21:24-27

JESUS SAYS -- "<u>I AM COMING SOON</u>" -- Trust Him -- Revelation 22:7

"So be it -- <u>COME LORD JESUS</u>"
Revelation 22:20-24

<u>TO GOD BE ALL THE GLORY</u>

Foreword

Leo Wehrspann's *"A Bible Reading Guide for Bible Reading People"* is indeed a valuable tool for individuals desiring to study the scriptures chronologically. A chronological study of the scriptures will certainly enhance the reader's understanding of the scriptures as the "history" of God's action in the life of his people. Even though there may be some difference of opinion among theologians concerning the precise accurateness of the chronology presented, this will provide no obstacle for the individual whose primary intent is to grow in his general understanding of the Bible as history.

Pastor Wehrspann provides his readers with an excellent aide in the section entitled *"Reflections on Readings."* It is particularly interesting to note that this section is indeed committed to assisting the reader with "reflections." The intent is obviously not to "instruct" the reader, but rather to help the reader "reflect" on the meaning and application of the text.

In addition to providing the Bible students utilizing this study with some very helpful materials in understanding the scriptures as history, the author also provides the student with help in understanding scriptures as "law and gospel." This emphasis will certainly be most helpful to the student as he/she reflects on the implications of the message in his/her personal life.

An additional help provided by the author is the occasional inclusion of material to assist the student in understanding the content of a particular portion of scripture. The *"Chronological History of the Kings and Prophets of the Divided Kingdom"* is an excellent example of such helpful material.

The "Bible Reading People" who utilize this "Bible Study Guide" will undoubtedly grow not only in their understanding of the chronological sequence of the scriptures, but also grow in their knowledge of Him who is the central focus of the scriptures — Jesus Christ.

Sincerely,

Harold Kieschnick

Harold Kieschnick
Executive Secretary
Parish Services
The Southern District
of the Lutheran Church —
Missouri Synod

Dedicated to:

Helen, loving wife, faithful companion,
woman of grace

Bob McConnell, the Pastor's Pastor,
lay priest par excellence

Rene' Carpentier, friend, companion,
confidant, leader of God's people

Sieg & Louise Rein, friends in faith,
and in fellowship with Christ
and His people

Copyright © 1990 by
Rev. Leo E. Wehrspann

7719 / ISBN 1-55673-215-5

PRINTED IN U.S.A.

A BIBLE READING GUIDE
FOR
BIBLE READING PEOPLE

by
Rev. Leo E. Wehrspann
1990

To
Dolores
Peace thru the WORD!
Pastor Wehrspann
7/17/92